# CORPSE TALK

## Groundbreaking

# WOMEN

BY ADAM AND LISA MURPHY

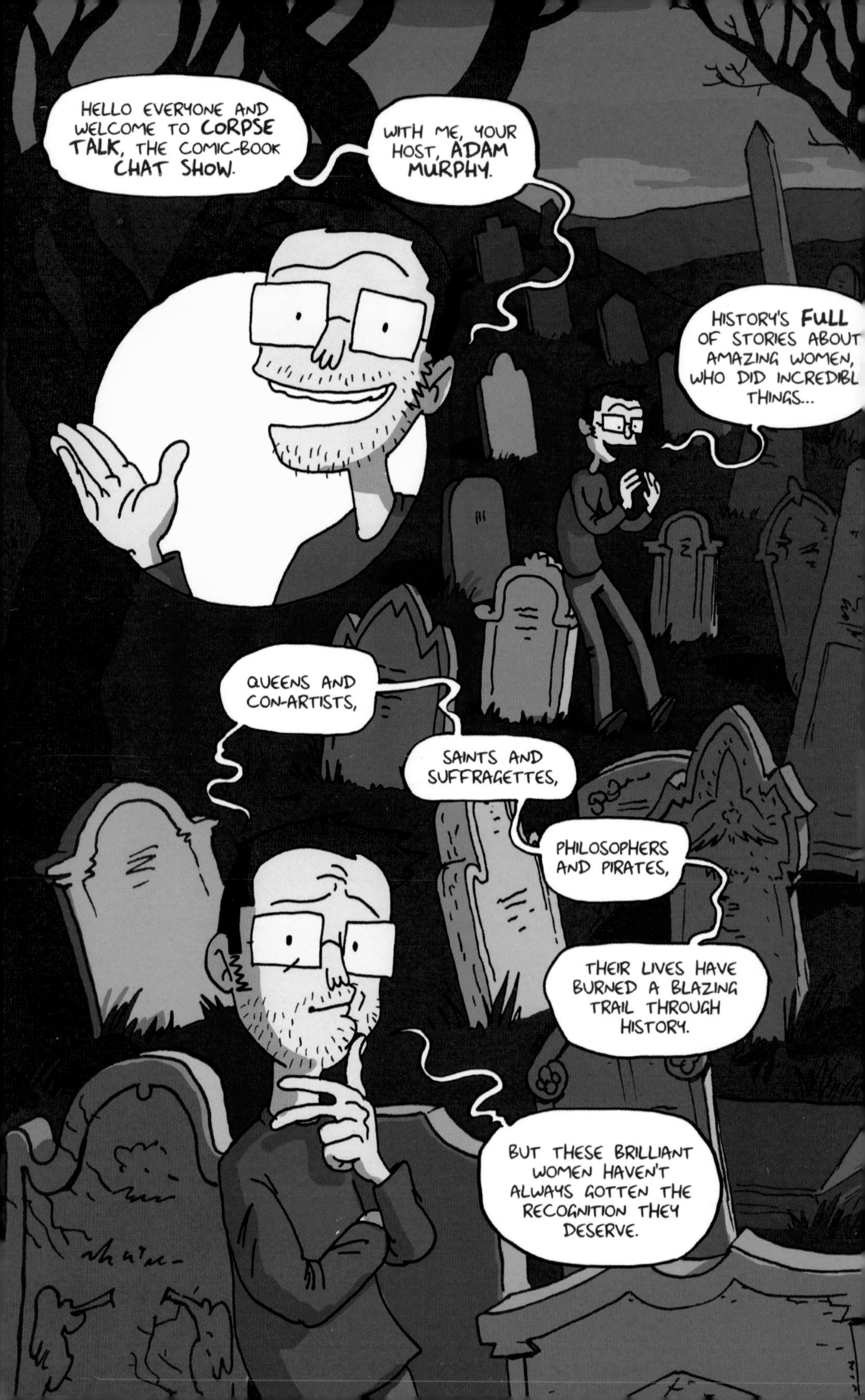
HELLO EVERYONE AND WELCOME TO CORPSE TALK, THE COMIC-BOOK CHAT SHOW.
WITH ME, YOUR HOST, ADAM MURPHY.
HISTORY'S FULL OF STORIES ABOUT AMAZING WOMEN, WHO DID INCREDIBL THINGS...
QUEENS AND CON-ARTISTS,
SAINTS AND SUFFRAGETTES,
PHILOSOPHERS AND PIRATES,
THEIR LIVES HAVE BURNED A BLAZING TRAIL THROUGH HISTORY.
BUT THESE BRILLIANT WOMEN HAVEN'T ALWAYS GOTTEN THE RECOGNITION THEY DESERVE.

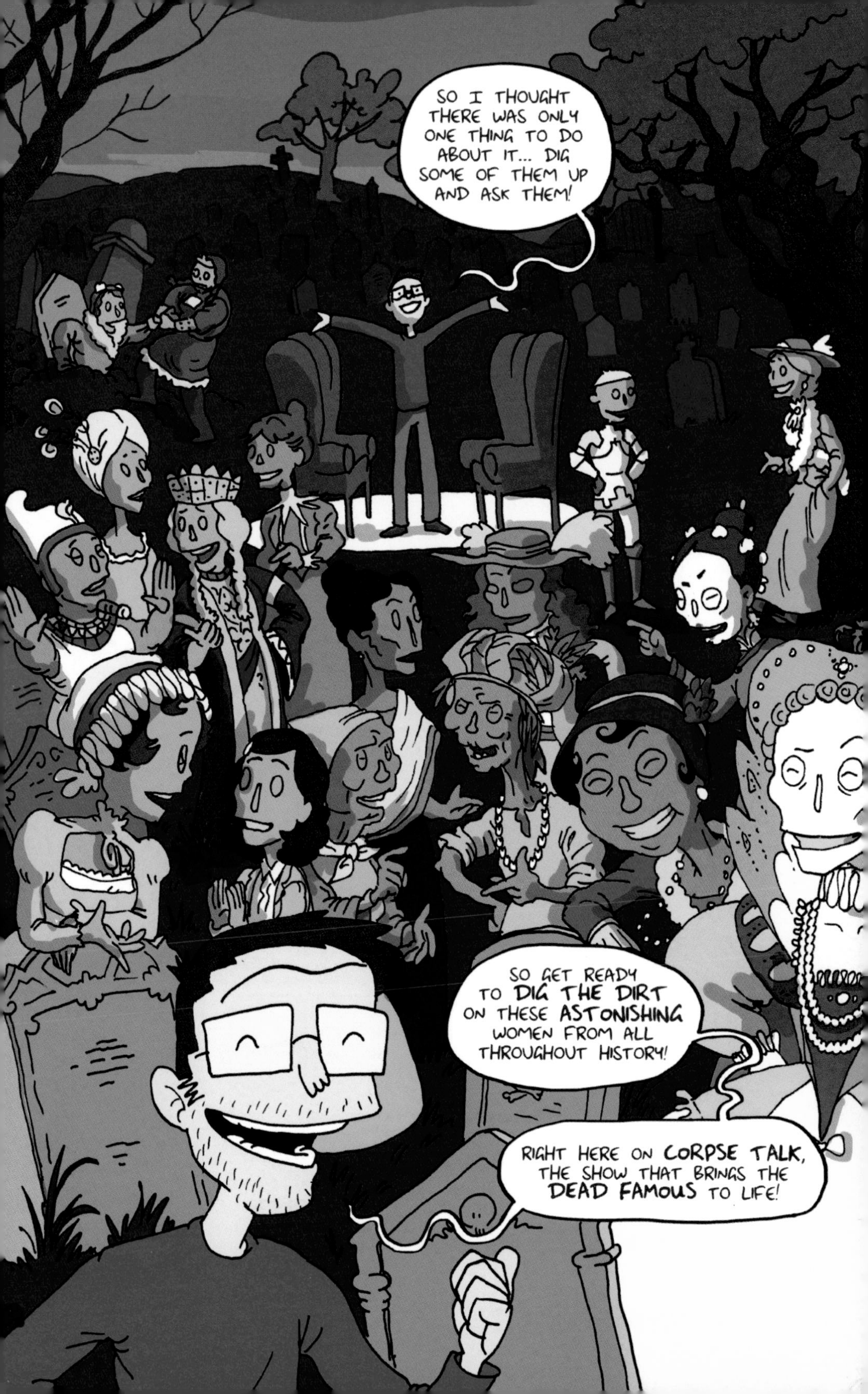
SO I THOUGHT THERE WAS ONLY ONE THING TO DO ABOUT IT... DIG SOME OF THEM UP AND ASK THEM!
SO GET READY TO DIG THE DIRT ON THESE ASTONISHING WOMEN FROM ALL THROUGHOUT HISTORY!
RIGHT HERE ON CORPSE TALK, THE SHOW THAT BRINGS THE DEAD FAMOUS TO LIFE!

# CONTENTS

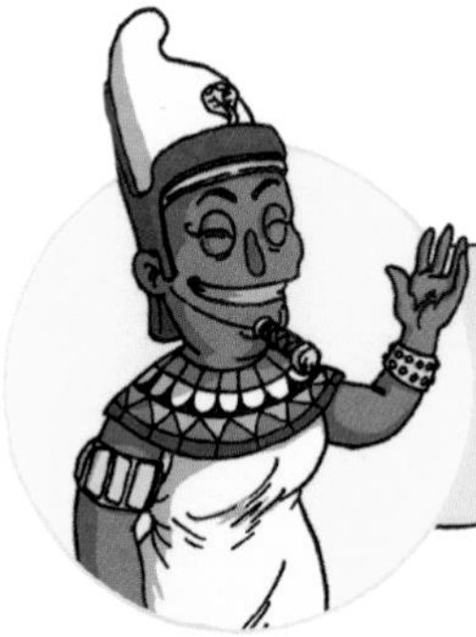
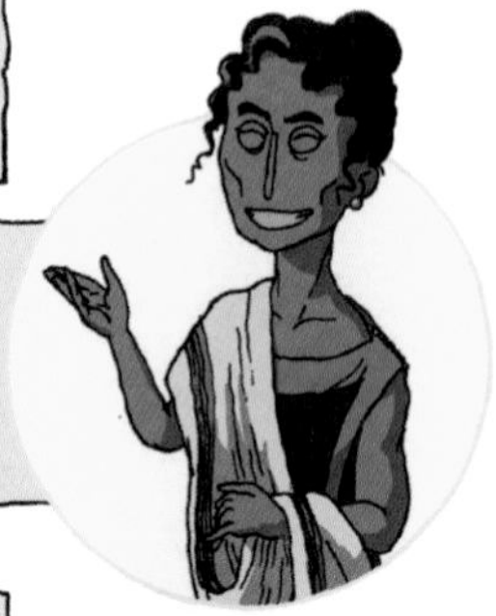
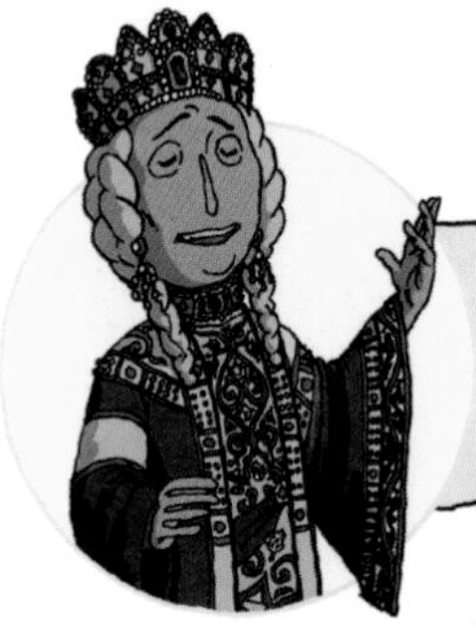
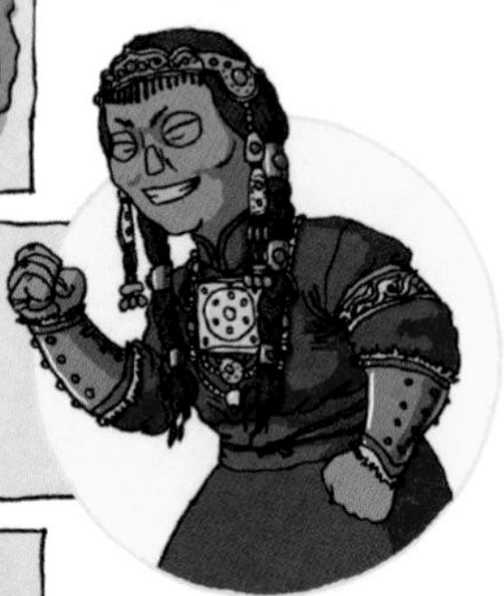
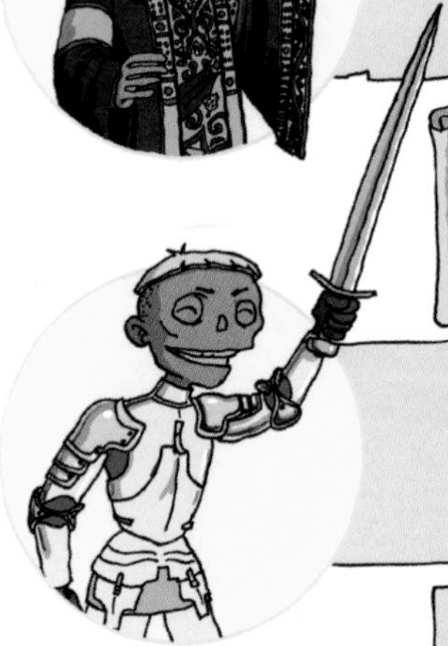
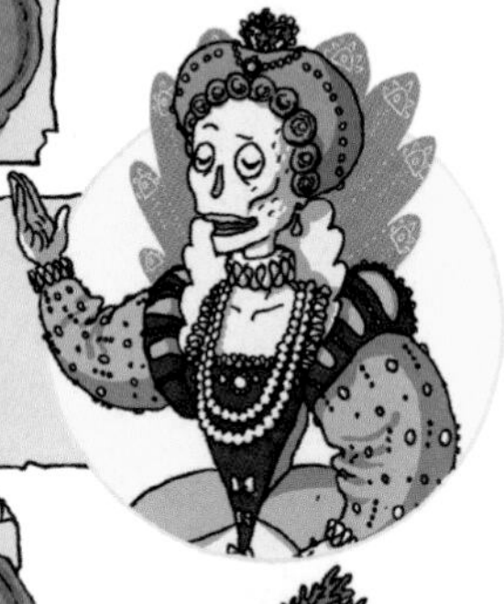
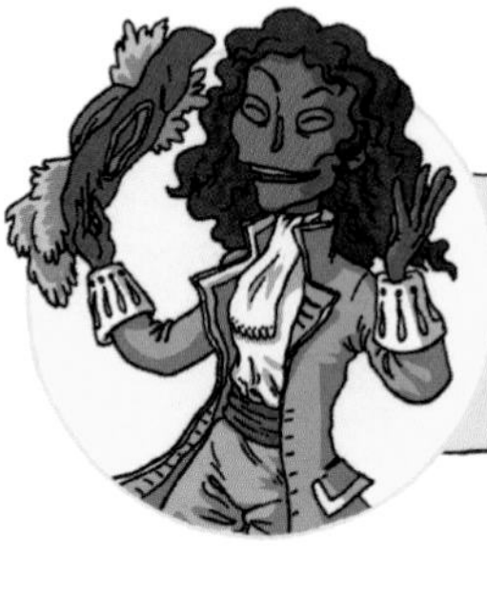
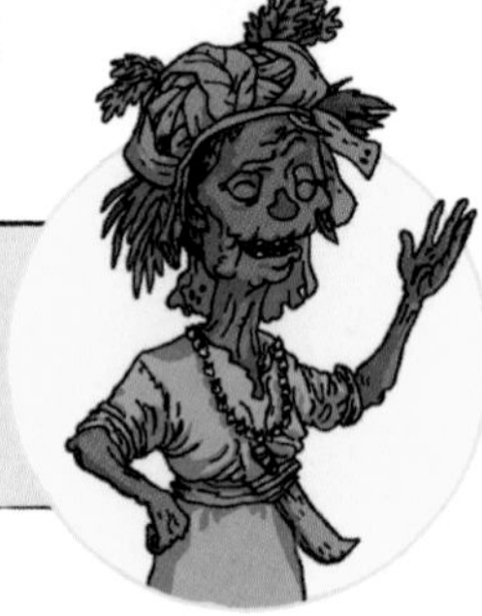

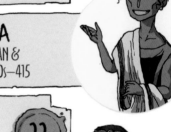

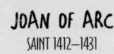

**JANE AUSTEN** 58
NOVELIST 1775–1817

**CHING SHIH** 66
PIRATE QUEEN 1775–1844

**PRINCESS CARABOO** 72
CON ARTIST 1791–1864

**HARRIET TUBMAN** 80
ABOLITIONIST 1822–1913

86 **EMILY DAVISON**
SUFFRAGETTE 1872–1913

**NELLIE BLY** 96
JOURNALIST 1864–1922

102 **AMY JOHNSON**
AVIATOR 1903–1941

**ANNE FRANK** 108
DIARIST 1929–1945

114 **JOSEPHINE BAKER**
ENTERTAINER 1906–1975

MY FIRST GUEST IS ALSO THE **FIRST LADY OF HISTORY**—QUITE LITERALLY! SHE'S ONE OF THE FIRST WOMEN WE REALLY KNOW **ANYTHING** ABOUT! AND WHAT A WOMAN...

IT'S THE FEMALE PHARAOH, THE JEWEL OF THE NILE... PLEASE WELCOME HER MAJESTY THE KING...

# HATSHEPSUT!

HATSHEPSUT
PHARAOH
1507–1458 BCE

HATSHEPSUT, YOUR EXTRA-ORDINARY CAREER WAS ALMOST **UNIQUE** IN THE HISTORY OF ANCIENT EGYPT, OVERTURNING CENTURIES OF TRADITION TO BECOME THE GREATEST **FEMALE PHARAOH** EVER!

I LIKE TO THINK I WAS ONE OF THE GREATEST PHARAOHS, **PERIOD.** NEVER MIND THE "FEMALE" BIT...

OH, RIGHT—SORRY. OF **COURSE** THAT'S WHAT I MEAN...

BUT STILL, IT'S PRETTY IMPRESSIVE CONSIDERING JUST **HOW** OPPOSED THE ANCIENT EGYPTIANS WERE TO WOMEN RULERS...

IN MORE THAN **3 MILLENNIA** OF PHARAOHS, YOU CAN COUNT THE WOMEN ON ONE HAND!

EH. THE EGYPTIANS WERE REALLY INTO **TRADITION**.

THEY BELIEVED YOU HAD TO DO THINGS **EXACTLY** AS THEY'D ALWAYS BEEN DONE, OR THE GODS WOULD BE ANGRY.

OFFERINGS ARE A BIT **LATE** TODAY...

SMITE 'EM.

NOT ONLY THAT, THE **LAST** TIME WE HAD A FEMALE RULER, THE KINGDOM WAS INVADED BY BARBARIANS...

NOT THAT IT WAS **HER FAULT**, POOR DEAR, BUT WHEN THINGS GO WRONG PEOPLE TEND TO LOOK FOR SOMEONE TO BLAME...

WELL, THERE'S REALLY A **RANGE** OF SOCIO-HISTORICAL FACTORS AT PLAY HERE...

SO YOU DECIDED TO PROVE THOSE PATRIARCHAL PYRAMID-DWELLERS WRONG!

I'D SAY IT'S MORE LIKE I DIDN'T HAVE A CHOICE...

MY HUSBAND, THE PREVIOUS PHARAOH, DIED YOUNG, LEAVING MY TWO-YEAR-OLD STEPSON AS THE NEXT RULER...

**SOMEBODY** HAD TO TAKE CHARGE, SO THAT'S WHAT I DID, RULING AS **REGENT**—A SORT OF PHARAOH STAND-IN.

GOO, GOO!

HIS MAJESTY SAYS: **5%** TAX ON ALL SHIPPING...

BUT A BABY PHARAOH WAS **ALSO** NOT HOW THINGS WERE DONE...

PAH! **I'D** BE A BETTER PHARAOH THAN THAT KID!

Y'KNOW, ACCIDENTS **DO** HAPPEN...

WITH THE VULTURES CIRCLING, WE NEEDED A GROWN-UP PHARAOH, AND **FAST!** I DECIDED IT WAS MY TIME TO SHINE...

SO I STARTED A LEGEND THAT I WAS ACTUALLY THE CHILD OF THE GREAT GOD **AMUN-RA**, SLAPPED ON A FAKE BEARD AND DECLARED **MYSELF** PHARAOH!

YEAH, I'VE BEEN MEANING TO ASK: WHAT **IS** THE DEAL WITH THAT BEARD, WAS IT TO DISGUISE YOURSELF AS A MAN?

COME ON. THEY WEREN'T **BLIND**...

I TOLD YOU: THE EGYPTIANS WERE REAL STICKLERS FOR TRADITION! THE PHARAOH **TRADITIONALLY** WORE A FAKE BEARD, SO THAT'S JUST WHAT I DID.

WELL, I GUESS THAT'S OK THEN...

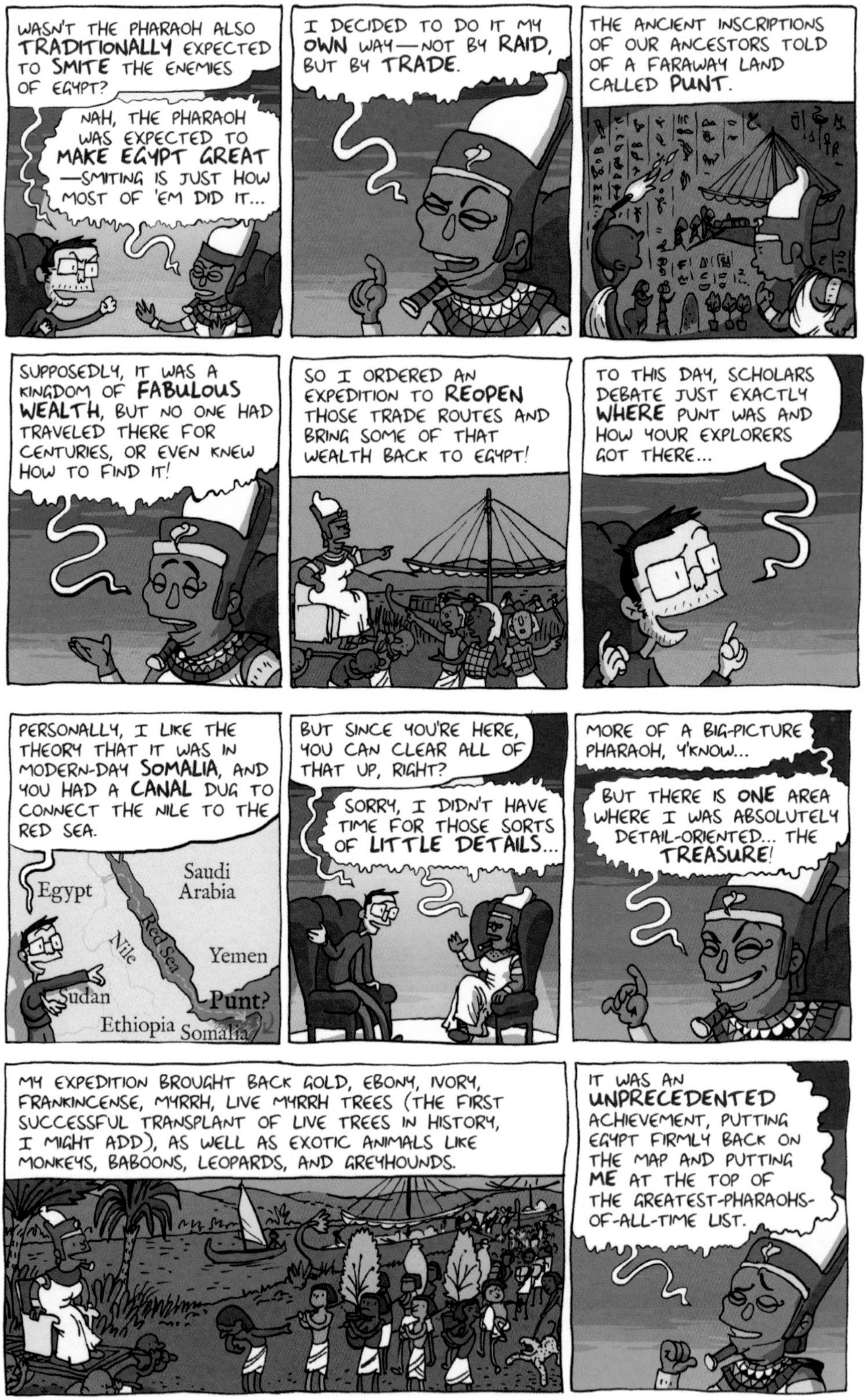
WASN'T THE PHARAOH ALSO TRADITIONALLY EXPECTED TO SMITE THE ENEMIES OF EGYPT?
NAH, THE PHARAOH WAS EXPECTED TO MAKE EGYPT GREAT —SMITING IS JUST HOW MOST OF 'EM DID IT...
I DECIDED TO DO IT MY OWN WAY—NOT BY RAID, BUT BY TRADE.
THE ANCIENT INSCRIPTIONS OF OUR ANCESTORS TOLD OF A FARAWAY LAND CALLED PUNT.
SUPPOSEDLY, IT WAS A KINGDOM OF FABULOUS WEALTH, BUT NO ONE HAD TRAVELED THERE FOR CENTURIES, OR EVEN KNEW HOW TO FIND IT!
SO I ORDERED AN EXPEDITION TO REOPEN THOSE TRADE ROUTES AND BRING SOME OF THAT WEALTH BACK TO EGYPT!
TO THIS DAY, SCHOLARS DEBATE JUST EXACTLY WHERE PUNT WAS AND HOW YOUR EXPLORERS GOT THERE...
PERSONALLY, I LIKE THE THEORY THAT IT WAS IN MODERN-DAY SOMALIA, AND YOU HAD A CANAL DUG TO CONNECT THE NILE TO THE RED SEA.
Egypt
Saudi Arabia
Nile
Red Sea
Yemen
Sudan
Punt?
Ethiopia
Somalia
BUT SINCE YOU'RE HERE, YOU CAN CLEAR ALL OF THAT UP, RIGHT?
SORRY, I DIDN'T HAVE TIME FOR THOSE SORTS OF LITTLE DETAILS...
MORE OF A BIG-PICTURE PHARAOH, Y'KNOW...
BUT THERE IS ONE AREA WHERE I WAS ABSOLUTELY DETAIL-ORIENTED... THE TREASURE!
MY EXPEDITION BROUGHT BACK GOLD, EBONY, IVORY, FRANKINCENSE, MYRRH, LIVE MYRRH TREES (THE FIRST SUCCESSFUL TRANSPLANT OF LIVE TREES IN HISTORY, I MIGHT ADD), AS WELL AS EXOTIC ANIMALS LIKE MONKEYS, BABOONS, LEOPARDS, AND GREYHOUNDS.
IT WAS AN UNPRECEDENTED ACHIEVEMENT, PUTTING EGYPT FIRMLY BACK ON THE MAP AND PUTTING ME AT THE TOP OF THE GREATEST-PHARAOHS-OF-ALL-TIME LIST.

WITH ALL THAT NEWFOUND WEALTH, YOU WERE ABLE TO ACCOMPLISH THAT **OTHER** GOAL OF A GREAT PHARAOH: BUILDING GIGANTIC MONUMENTS!

SPECTACULAR TEMPLES, MASSIVE OBELISKS, HUGE STATUES OF MYSELF: YOU NAME IT, I BUILT IT!

AT MY GREATEST TEMPLE COMPLEX, I HAD **200** GIANT SPHINXES WITH **MY** HEAD ON 'EM!

THAT WAY I COULD BE SURE MY LEGACY WAS SECURE AND NO ONE WOULD EVER FORGET MY AWESOME ACHIEVEMENTS.

AH... WELL... ABOUT THAT... I'M NOT QUITE SURE HOW TO SAY THIS, BUT...

WHAT? **WHAT!?**

WELL, YOU REMEMBER THE BABY PHARAOH...? WHOSE THRONE YOU **USURPED?**

USURPED!? YOU MEAN SAVED!? OK, HE HAD TO SHARE WITH HIS STEP-MOTHER, BUT IT WAS ONLY THANKS TO ME HE STILL **HAD** A THRONE!

YEAH, WELL, HE DOESN'T SEEM TO HAVE FELT THE SAME WAY, SINCE AFTER YOU DIED HE HAD YOUR NAME **CHISELED OFF** ALL THOSE MONUMENTS, AND REPLACED WITH HIS OWN.

HE **WHAAT!?**

I GUESS THE EGYPTIANS HAD THE **TRADITION** OF MEN TAKING CREDIT FOR WOMEN'S WORK, TOO...

WHY, OF ALL THE UNGRATEFUL, BACKSTABBING, MUTTER MUTTER...

# TEMPLE COMPLEX

NOW IT'S TIME FOR HATSHEPSUT TO TELL US ALL ABOUT THAT MOST **ICONIC** OF EGYPTIAN EDIFICES, THE TRIANGULAR TEMPLE-TOMB OF THE PHARAOH, HER **PYRAMID!**

PSHAW! PYRAMIDS ARE SO **OLD KINGDOM!** I FOLLOWED THE **NEW** FASHION FOR **SECRET** TOMBS IN THE HIDDEN VALLEY OF THE KINGS.

HARDER FOR **GRAVE ROBBERS** TO FIND YOUR TREASURES WHEN YOU DON'T HAVE A MASSIVE **SIGNPOST** ABOVE YOUR GRAVE...

**200** STONE **SPHINXES** WITH **MY HEAD** ON THEM LINED THE WALKWAY FROM THE NEARBY CITY OF THEBES. JUST TO GET PEOPLE IN THE MOOD ON THEIR WAY HERE.

ON THE **SECOND LEVEL** WAS THE SHRINE OF THE COW GODDESS, **HATHOR.** SINCE I'M ONE OF HER FAVORITES, I'M HAVING A LITTLE DRINK FROM ONE OF HER UDDERS. PRETTY DEFINITE PROOF OF DIVINE FAVOR, IF YOU ASK ME.

THE **LOWER COURTYARD** WAS FILLED WITH EXOTIC **MYRRH** TREES AND OTHER STRANGE PLANTS BROUGHT BACK BY MY EXPEDITION TO THE FARAWAY LAND OF **PUNT.**

IT ALSO FEATURED SOME **MASSIVE STATUES** OF ME LOOKING LIKE A BOSS.

THERE'S ALSO **ANOTHER** TEMPLE BUILT BY AN EARLIER AND LESS AWESOME PHAROAH NEXT DOOR—IT'S PRETTY MUCH JUST THERE TO MAKE **MY TEMPLE** LOOK **EVEN MORE** MAGNIFICENT...

MY STEPSON, THE UNGRATEFUL JERK, HAD THEM DESTROYED, **AND** SCRATCHED MY FACE OFF ALL THE TEMPLE WALL PAINTINGS. COULDN'T HANDLE THE **AWESOME,** I GUESS.

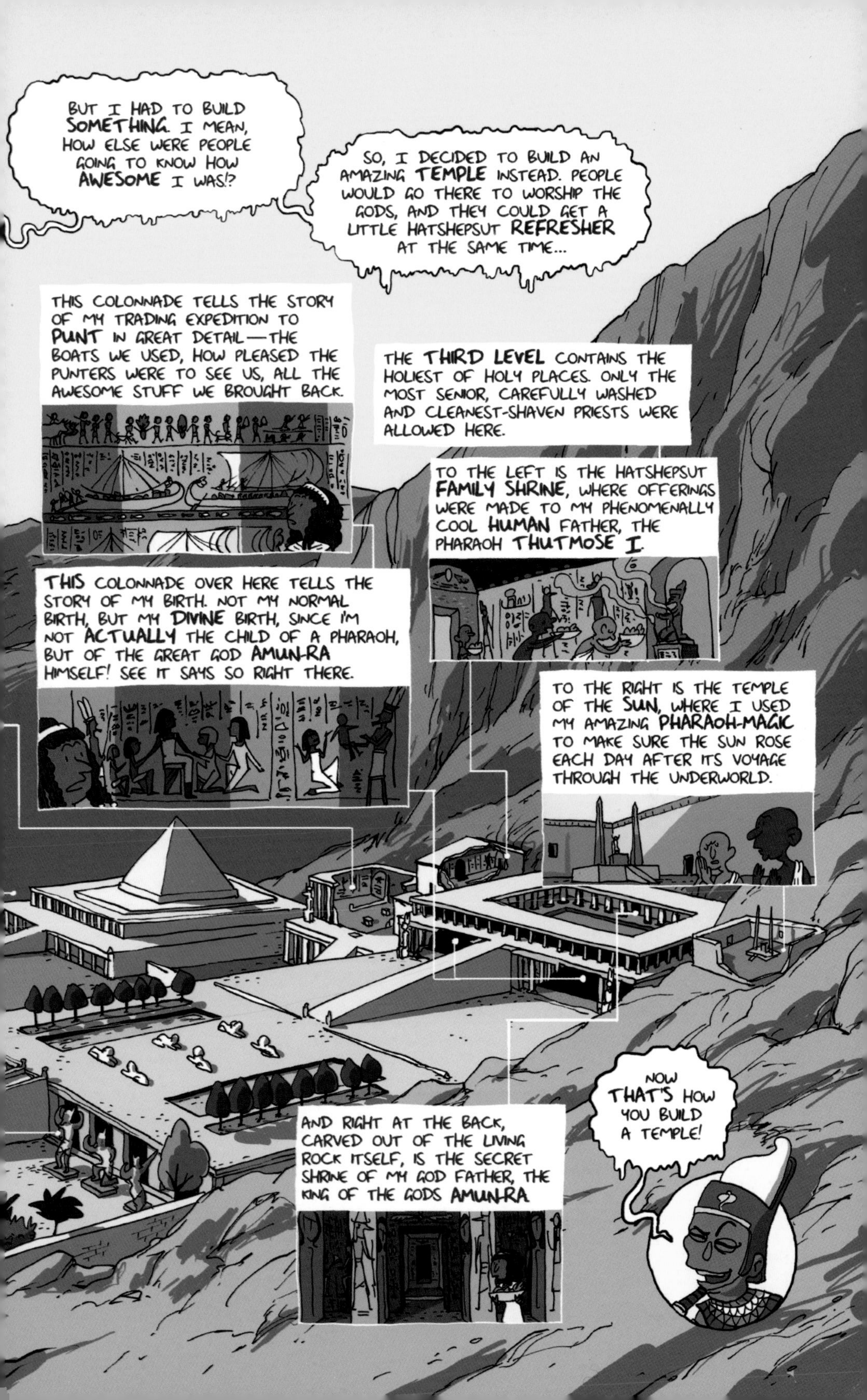
BUT I HAD TO BUILD SOMETHING. I MEAN, HOW ELSE WERE PEOPLE GOING TO KNOW HOW AWESOME I WAS!?
SO, I DECIDED TO BUILD AN AMAZING TEMPLE INSTEAD. PEOPLE WOULD GO THERE TO WORSHIP THE GODS, AND THEY COULD GET A LITTLE HATSHEPSUT REFRESHER AT THE SAME TIME...
THIS COLONNADE TELLS THE STORY OF MY TRADING EXPEDITION TO PUNT IN GREAT DETAIL—THE BOATS WE USED, HOW PLEASED THE PUNTERS WERE TO SEE US, ALL THE AWESOME STUFF WE BROUGHT BACK.
THE THIRD LEVEL CONTAINS THE HOLIEST OF HOLY PLACES. ONLY THE MOST SENIOR, CAREFULLY WASHED AND CLEANEST-SHAVEN PRIESTS WERE ALLOWED HERE.
TO THE LEFT IS THE HATSHEPSUT FAMILY SHRINE, WHERE OFFERINGS WERE MADE TO MY PHENOMENALLY COOL HUMAN FATHER, THE PHARAOH THUTMOSE I.
THIS COLONNADE OVER HERE TELLS THE STORY OF MY BIRTH. NOT MY NORMAL BIRTH, BUT MY DIVINE BIRTH, SINCE I'M NOT ACTUALLY THE CHILD OF A PHARAOH, BUT OF THE GREAT GOD AMUN-RA HIMSELF! SEE IT SAYS SO RIGHT THERE.
TO THE RIGHT IS THE TEMPLE OF THE SUN, WHERE I USED MY AMAZING PHARAOH-MAGIC TO MAKE SURE THE SUN ROSE EACH DAY AFTER ITS VOYAGE THROUGH THE UNDERWORLD.
AND RIGHT AT THE BACK, CARVED OUT OF THE LIVING ROCK ITSELF, IS THE SECRET SHRINE OF MY GOD FATHER, THE KING OF THE GODS AMUN-RA.
NOW THAT'S HOW YOU BUILD A TEMPLE!

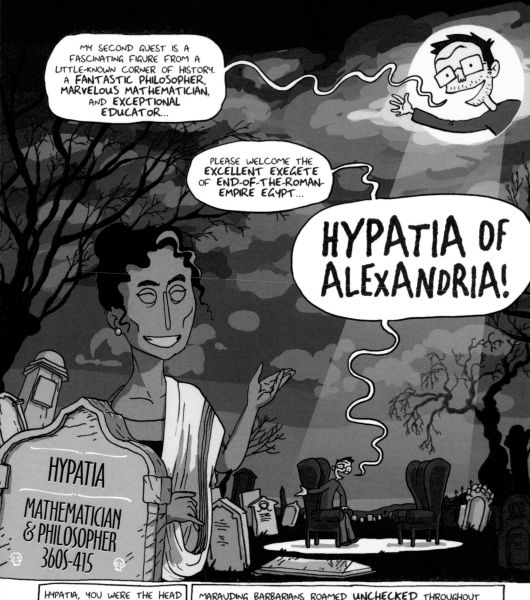

MY SECOND GUEST IS A FASCINATING FIGURE FROM A LITTLE-KNOWN CORNER OF HISTORY. A FANTASTIC PHILOSOPHER, MARVELOUS MATHEMATICIAN, AND EXCEPTIONAL EDUCATOR...

PLEASE WELCOME THE **EXCELLENT EXEGETE** OF **END-OF-THE-ROMAN-EMPIRE EGYPT**...

# HYPATIA OF ALEXANDRIA!

HYPATIA

MATHEMATICIAN & PHILOSOPHER 360S-415

HYPATIA, YOU WERE THE HEAD OF THE ANCIENT SCHOOL OF NEO-PLATONIC PHILOSOPHY IN **ALEXANDRIA**, THE CAPITAL OF EGYPT, DURING THE CHAOTIC YEARS LEADING UP TO THE **FALL OF THE ROMAN EMPIRE**...

MARAUDING BARBARIANS ROAMED **UNCHECKED** THROUGHOUT THE EMPIRE, EVEN GOING SO FAR AS TO **SACK** THE ETERNAL CITY OF **ROME ITSELF!**

YEAH, IT WAS A PRETTY DREADFUL TIME, FRANKLY. MORE THAN **1,000** YEARS OF CIVILIZATION AND CULTURE WAS GOING **UP IN SMOKE.**

QUITE LITERALLY. MY **DAD'S** PHILOSOPHY SCHOOL GOT BURNED DOWN BY AN ANGRY CHRISTIAN MOB.

HM. WHAT WERE THEY SO MAD ABOUT?

WELL, CHRISTIANITY HAD ONLY JUST BECOME THE OFFICIAL RELIGION OF THE ROMAN EMPIRE, REPLACING ALL THE OLD GODS LIKE JUPITER, MARS, VENUS, AND SO ON...

AND THEY DIDN'T WANT ANY RIVAL RELIGIONS, ESPECIALLY NOT THE OLD PAGAN GODS. SO THEY SMASHED UP THE OLD TEMPLES AND MADE THEM INTO CHURCHES.

ONE TEMPLE WAS IN THE SAME BUILDING AS DAD'S SCHOOL. OLD-GOD LOYALISTS **BARRICADED** THEMSELVES INSIDE TO DEFEND THEIR SACRED STATUES, SO THE MOB TORCHED THE PLACE.

WE GOT OUT IN TIME, BUT THE SCHOOL LIBRARY, WHICH HAD ONCE BEEN ONE OF THE **WONDERS OF THE WORLD,** WAS REDUCED TO ASHES.

ARRGH! JUST THINK OF ALL THOSE AMAZING BOOKS WE'LL **NEVER** GET TO READ!

POOR DAD COULDN'T HANDLE THE LOSS; HE DIED SOON AFTER. SO I TOOK OVER AS HEAD OF THE SCHOOL AND DEDICATED MY LIFE TO PRESERVING WHAT KNOWLEDGE I COULD.

OF COURSE THAT MEANS **TEACHING,** EXPLAINING THE ANCIENT CLASSICS FOR A MODERN AUDIENCE.

I'D HARDLY CALL THE **ROMAN EMPIRE** "MODERN."

NO, SURE, BUT SOME OF THESE BOOKS WERE ALREADY **HUNDREDS** OF YEARS OLD! IT'D BE LIKE YOU TRYING TO READ SHAKESPEARE OR SOMETHING—YOU MIGHT NEED SOME HELP...

UH. FAIR ENOUGH.

I TAUGHT ASTRONOMY, THE STUDY OF HOW THE SUN, STARS, AND PLANETS MOVE AROUND THE EARTH.

SUN EARTH

DOME OF FIXED STARS

OK, OK, I HEARD YOU HAVE A NEW SYSTEM NOW WITH THE **EARTH** GOING AROUND THE **SUN,** BUT OUR SYSTEM WAS **REMARKABLY ACCURATE** FOR IT'S TIME...

OF COURSE, ALL OF THIS WAS CONDEMNED BY THE MORE **INTOLERANT** CHRISTIANS AS ASTROLOGY, FORTUNE-TELLING, AND **MAGIC**...

AHA! SORCERY!

I ALSO TAUGHT **PHILOSOPHY**; USING REASON AND CAREFUL THOUGHT TO TRY AND FIGURE OUT THE NATURE OF **REALITY ITSELF**...

WHICH WAS CONDEMNED BY THE CHRISTIANS FOR TEACHING PEOPLE TO USE THEIR **MINDS** INSTEAD OF JUST FOLLOWING THEIR BISHOP.

HM. I'M STARTING TO DETECT A **PATTERN** HERE...

AND, OF COURSE, ME BEING A WOMAN **REALLY DIDN'T** HELP...

LOOK! THESE MEN ARE **LISTENING** TO HER!

THEY'RE... **RESPECTING** HER OPINIONS!

MUST BE SORCERY...

BUT MY GREAT PASSION WAS **MATH**!

OH, WONDERFUL MATH! HOW DO I LOVE THEE, LET ME COUNT THE WAYS...

1, 2, $\sqrt{2}$...

THAT WAS A MATH JOKE.

OH.

RIGHT.

DON'T **YOU** START! MATH IS AMAZING! WITH MATH YOU CAN KNOW THINGS THAT ARE **ABSOLUTELY** AND **PERFECTLY** TRUE!

NOT LIKE IN THE CRUMMY "**REAL**" WORLD, WHERE IT'S ALL "POSSIBLY" AND "TO THE BEST OF OUR KNOWLEDGE" AND "WELL, I THINK I READ IT ON THE INTERNET ONCE"...

MY SCHOOL, THE **NEO-PLATONISTS**, TAUGHT THAT THE ONLY **REALLY** REAL THINGS ARE IDEAS. AND THE MOST PERFECT IDEAS OF ALL ARE **MATHEMATICAL** ONES.

SO, LET ME GUESS, THE CHRISTIANS CONDEMNED THE MATH, TOO.

OH, YEAH. ALTHOUGH DON'T GET ME WRONG— NOT **ALL** OF THEM WERE LIKE THAT...

SOME CHRISTIANS WERE VERY INTERESTED IN MATH AND PHILOSOPHY. AND EVEN **COMBINED** THEM WITH CHRISTIAN TEACHINGS TO MAKE A RICHER AND MORE COMPELLING RELIGION.

AND LOTS OF THEM WERE KIND. LIKE, THEY WENT AROUND FORGIVING AND CARING FOR PEOPLE, EVEN THOSE PEOPLE THEY DISAGREED WITH...

BUT ANCIENT ALEXANDRIA WAS JUST PARTICULARLY WELL SUPPLIED WITH **ANGRY MOBS**, CHRISTIAN OR OTHERWISE.

WHICH WAS KIND OF A DRAG. I MEAN, IT'S NOT EASY TRYING TO UNTANGLE THE **ABSOLUTE NATURE OF REALITY** WITH **ROCKS** PELTING THROUGH YOUR WINDOWS ALL THE TIME.

ROCKS THAT MAY OR MAY NOT ACTUALLY BE REAL...

BONK!

THE **CITY GOVERNOR** WAS TRYING TO MAKE EVERYONE PLAY NICE (AND GOT PELTED BY A MOB OF ANGRY MONKS FOR HIS TROUBLE).

HE WAS THE TOLERANT-AND-INTERESTED-IN-PHILOSOPHY TYPE OF CHRISTIAN. USED TO ASK MY ADVICE ON ALL SORTS OF STUFF.

HYPATIA, WHAT AM I TO DO WITH ALL THESE MOBS...?

WHICH TURNED OUT TO BE KIND OF A PROBLEM. THE MOB GOT WIND THAT I WAS ADVISING HIM AND BASICALLY BLAMED ME FOR EVERYTHING.

SHE'S **BEWITCHED** THE GOVERNOR!

YOU WERE GRABBED FROM YOUR CARRIAGE, DRAGGED TO A CHURCH, AND STONED TO DEATH WITH ROOF TILES.

WHY **ROOF TILES**?

DUNNO. MAYBE THEY WERE REDOING THE CHURCH ROOF? THAT'S SURELY NOT THE POINT.

SO WHAT **IS** THE POINT THEN? WHAT LESSONS **CAN** WE LEARN FROM YOUR GRUESOME DEATH?

HUH? HOW WOULD **I** KNOW?

NEVER TRUST AN ANGRY MOB? PROTECT WOMEN IN SCIENCE?

BEWARE OF CHURCHES UNDERGOING RENOVATION?

SEE, THIS IS WHY I LIKE **MATH**—AT LEAST WHEN **I** GET THE RIGHT ANSWER, I KNOW IT...

# THE GOLDEN RATIO

HYPATIA'S PHILOSOPHY SCHOOL TAUGHT THAT **NUMBERS** ARE THE **SECRET LANGUAGE** IN WHICH THE UNIVERSE IS WRITTEN.

AND THERE'S ONE AMAZING NUMBER IN PARTICULAR THAT HAS FASCINATED AND BEFUDDLED MATHEMATICIANS THROUGHOUT HISTORY—THE **GOLDEN RATIO!**

A **RATIO** IS A NUMBER THAT **COMPARES** TWO OTHER NUMBERS.

SO, FOR EXAMPLE, THIS LINE IS **TWICE** AS LONG AS THIS ONE.

WE SAY THE RATIO IS **2:1.**

YOU CAN MAYBE SEE IT BETTER IN A RECTANGLE. THE LONG SIDE IS TWICE AS LONG AS THE SHORT SIDE.

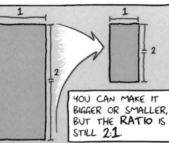

YOU CAN MAKE IT BIGGER OR SMALLER, BUT THE **RATIO** IS STILL **2:1.**

WELL, THE **GOLDEN** RATIO IS 1.61803398874989484820458683 4... :1!

THIS "..." MEANS IT KEEPS GOING FOREVER AND NEVER REPEATS ITSELF.

INSTEAD OF WRITING ALL THAT OUT, WE USE THE GREEK LETTER φ (PRONOUNCED "FIE").

φ HAS ALL SORTS OF WEIRD AND WONDERFUL MATHEMATICAL PROPERTIES...

BUT ITS ALSO SOMETHING THAT'S ALL AROUND US IN THE NATURAL WORLD!

TAKE A **PINE CONE**, FOR EXAMPLE (SEE IF YOU CAN FIND ONE AND DO THIS AT HOME)...

IF YOU COUNT THE SPIRALS YOU GET **13** GOING THIS WAY...

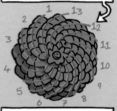

AND **8** THIS WAY.

SEE HOW THE LITTLE POINTED NUBBIN THINGS SPIRAL AROUND THE CONE?

USE A MARKER TO COLOR IN THE SPIRALS IF IT HELPS.

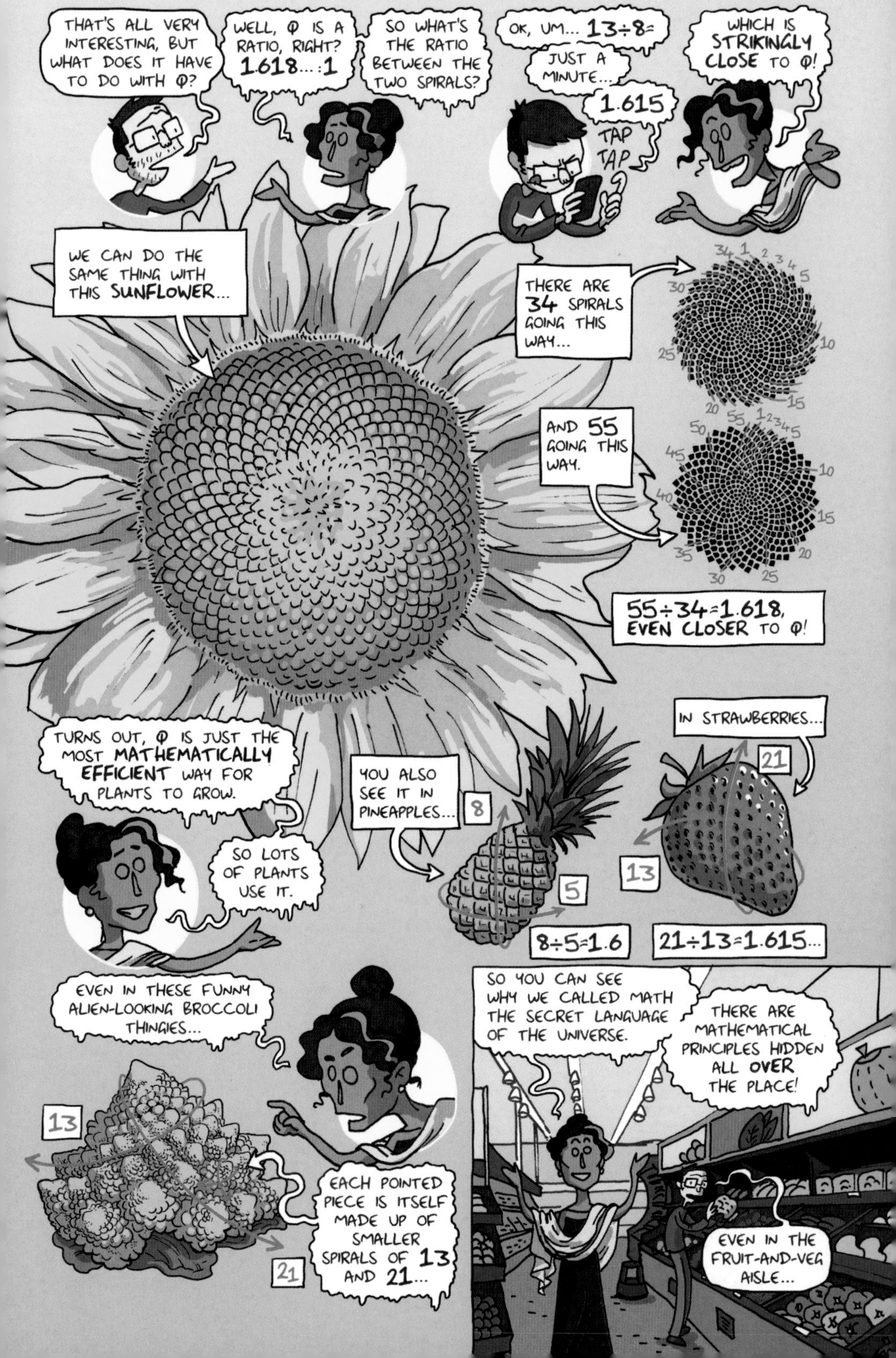
THAT'S ALL VERY INTERESTING, BUT WHAT DOES IT HAVE TO DO WITH φ?
WELL, φ IS A RATIO, RIGHT? 1.618....:1
SO WHAT'S THE RATIO BETWEEN THE TWO SPIRALS?
OK, UM... 13÷8=
JUST A MINUTE...
1.615
TAP TAP
WHICH IS STRIKINGLY CLOSE TO φ!
WE CAN DO THE SAME THING WITH THIS SUNFLOWER...
THERE ARE 34 SPIRALS GOING THIS WAY...
AND 55 GOING THIS WAY.
55÷34=1.618, EVEN CLOSER TO φ!
TURNS OUT, φ IS JUST THE MOST MATHEMATICALLY EFFICIENT WAY FOR PLANTS TO GROW.
SO LOTS OF PLANTS USE IT.
YOU ALSO SEE IT IN PINEAPPLES...
8
5
IN STRAWBERRIES...
21
13
8÷5=1.6
21÷13=1.615...
EVEN IN THESE FUNNY ALIEN-LOOKING BROCCOLI THINGIES...
13
21
EACH POINTED PIECE IS ITSELF MADE UP OF SMALLER SPIRALS OF 13 AND 21...
SO YOU CAN SEE WHY WE CALLED MATH THE SECRET LANGUAGE OF THE UNIVERSE.
THERE ARE MATHEMATICAL PRINCIPLES HIDDEN ALL OVER THE PLACE!
EVEN IN THE FRUIT-AND-VEG AISLE...

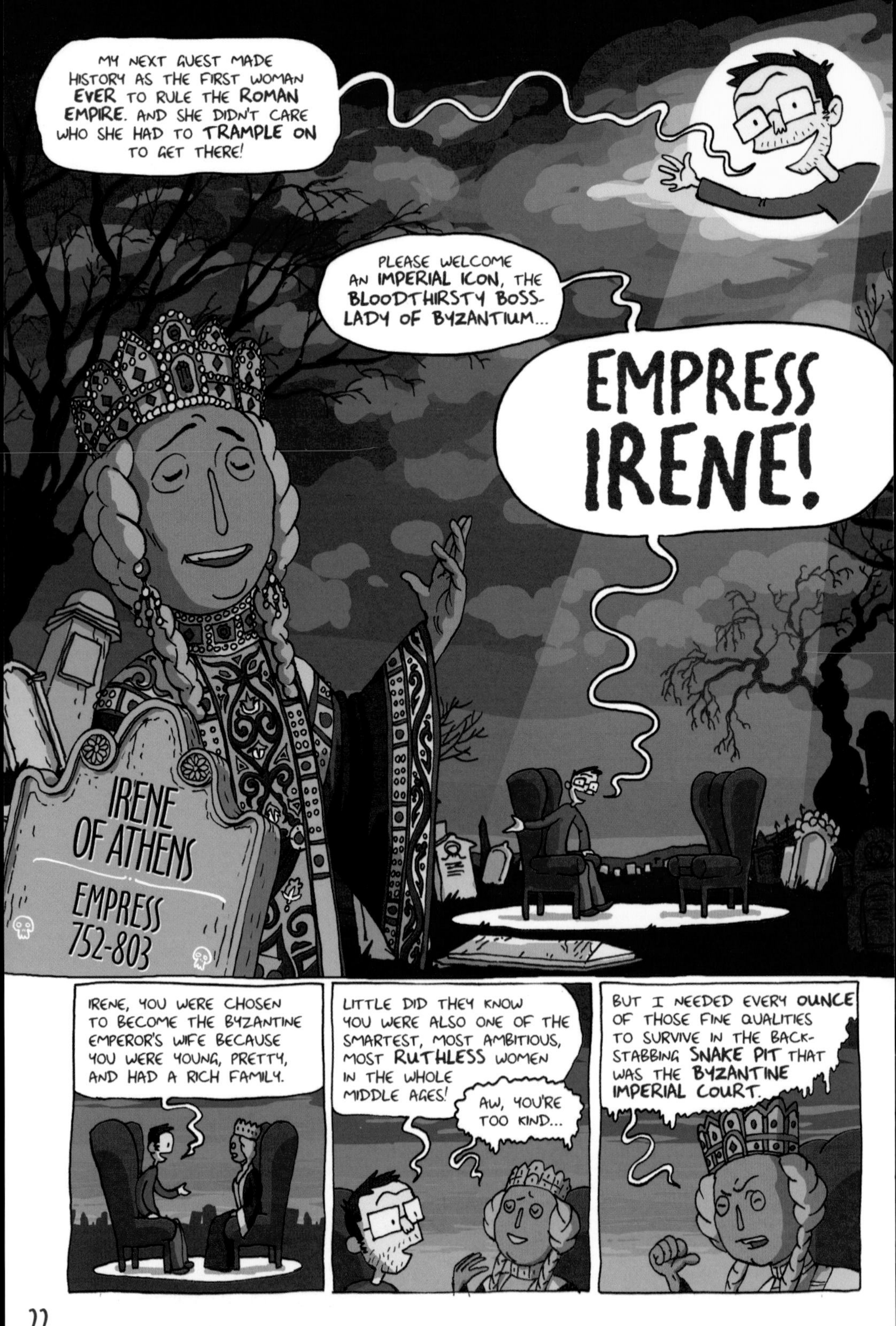
MY NEXT GUEST MADE HISTORY AS THE FIRST WOMAN EVER TO RULE THE ROMAN EMPIRE. AND SHE DIDN'T CARE WHO SHE HAD TO TRAMPLE ON TO GET THERE!
PLEASE WELCOME AN IMPERIAL ICON, THE BLOODTHIRSTY BOSS-LADY OF BYZANTIUM...
EMPRESS IRENE!
IRENE OF ATHENS
EMPRESS 752-803
IRENE, YOU WERE CHOSEN TO BECOME THE BYZANTINE EMPEROR'S WIFE BECAUSE YOU WERE YOUNG, PRETTY, AND HAD A RICH FAMILY.
LITTLE DID THEY KNOW YOU WERE ALSO ONE OF THE SMARTEST, MOST AMBITIOUS, MOST RUTHLESS WOMEN IN THE WHOLE MIDDLE AGES!
AW, YOU'RE TOO KIND...
BUT I NEEDED EVERY OUNCE OF THOSE FINE QUALITIES TO SURVIVE IN THE BACK-STABBING SNAKE PIT THAT WAS THE BYZANTINE IMPERIAL COURT.

AND THE FANGS **REALLY** CAME OUT WHEN THE EMPEROR DIED, LEAVING **YOU** TO RUN THE PLACE ON BEHALF OF YOUR **10-YEAR-OLD** SON, CONSTANTINE.

I'D ONLY BEEN IN CHARGE **6 WEEKS** WHEN SOME DUDE CAME ALONG DOING THE WHOLE DON'T-PUT-A-WOMAN-IN-CHARGE-I'D-BE-A-**MUCH**-BETTER-EMPEROR THING...

SO YOU HAD HIM RUTHLESSLY MURDERED?

**BETTER.** I RUTHLESSLY HAD HIM MADE A PRIEST.

PRIESTS COULDN'T BECOME EMPERORS, YOU SEE. **AND I** MADE HIM SERVE MASS ON CHRISTMAS DAY, IN FRONT OF THE WHOLE CITY, TO MAKE SURE EVERYONE KNEW IT.

WITH YOUR POWER SECURE, YOU BEGAN THE GREAT WORK OF YOUR REIGN—A CAMPAIGN TO RESTORE **ICONS.**

THESE ICONS WERE RELIGIOUS PICTURES OF SAINTS. THE LAST FEW EMPERORS HAD BEEN REALLY **DOWN** ON THEM, BANNING THEM FROM CHURCHES AND SO ON.

BUT WHY WOULD ANYONE OBJECT TO **RELIGIOUS PICTURES**? I MEAN, THIS WAS THE MIDDLE AGES, RIGHT? WASN'T EVERYONE SUPER RELIGIOUS BACK THEN?

SO SUPER RELIGIOUS...

HERE'S THE THING: THE BYZANTINE EMPIRE USED TO BE THE **ROMAN** EMPIRE, RIGHT? AND EVERYBODY KNOWS THE ROMANS RULED HALF THE KNOWN WORLD.

HAR, HAR!

ROMAN EMPIRE

BUT BY MY DAY, WE'D BEEN ON THE RECEIVING END OF A **400-YEAR-LONG BUTT-KICKING** THAT HAD REDUCED OUR TERRITORY TO BASICALLY WHAT IS NOW GREECE AND TURKEY.

GERMANIC BARBARIANS

ER...

BYZANTINE EMPIRE

ISLAMIC CALIPHATE

SO, PEOPLE STARTED TO WORRY THAT GOD WAS **ANGRY** ABOUT SOMETHING AND THAT WAS WHY HE WAS **LETTING** EVERYONE KICK OUR BUTTS.

ANGRY ABOUT WHAT?

THESE **ICONS**! THE THEORY WAS THAT MAYBE PEOPLE WERE WORSHIPING **THEM** TOO MUCH WHEN THEY **SHOULD** BE WORSHIPING GOD.

OR SOMETHING—IT NEVER MADE MUCH SENSE TO ME. I **LIKED** THE ICONS. I MEAN, COME ON—LOOK AT THIS CUTE LITTLE FACE!

PLUS, THEY WERE PART OF OUR HERITAGE. SO I HAD THE CHURCH DECLARE THAT THOSE PREVIOUS EMPERORS WERE **IDIOTS** AND PUT ALL THE ICONS BACK.

BUT THE **ARMY** WAS CONVINCED THIS WAS GOING TO LOSE THEM BATTLES AND SO THEY SCARED OFF THE CHURCHMEN.

AND RISK MAKING GOD ANGRY?

ARE YOU CRAZY?

THE NERVE! BUT I SOON SHOWED THEM. I INVENTED A FAKE REPORT ABOUT AN ENEMY INVASION TO GET THEM ALL OUT OF THE CAPITAL...

HMM, THEY **SHOULD** BE SOMEWHERE AROUND HERE...

BUT THEN, WHEN THEY GOT BACK, THEY FOUND I'D GIVEN THEIR JOBS TO NEW, MORE **LOYAL** SOLDIERS.

SORRY, BUB. EMPRESS'S ORDERS.

SOLDIERS WITH ORDERS TO **KILL THEIR FAMILIES** IF THEY CAUSED ME TROUBLE **EVER AGAIN.**

WOOF! THAT'S BRUTAL!

THANKS.

BUT I WAS JUST GETTING WARMED UP...

I HAD ONLY ONE PROBLEM. MY SON **CONSTANTINE** WAS GETTING OLD ENOUGH TO RULE FOR HIMSELF.

AND FOR SOME REASON, HE DIDN'T SEEM EAGER TO HAVE HIS MOM TELLING HIM WHAT TO DO FOR THE REST OF HIS LIFE.

**UNGRATEFUL** LITTLE UPSTART! HE EVEN HAD THE NERVE TO TRY AND OVERTHROW **ME**! I GROUNDED HIM GOOD FOR THAT!

GO TO YOUR PALACE AND THINK ABOUT WHAT YOU'VE DONE!

AFTER THAT, I HAD THE ARMY SWEAR AN OATH OF LOYALTY TO **ME**, PROMISING NOT TO MAKE THE LITTLE JERK EMPEROR WHILE I WAS STILL ALIVE.

BUT THAT PROVED TOO MUCH, EVEN FOR YOUR NEW SOLDIERS. THEY ROSE UP, CROWNED CONSTANTINE, AND RELEGATED YOU TO PLAIN OLD "EMPEROR'S MOM" AGAIN.

THAT MUST HAVE RANKLED...

IT RANKLED LIKE ALL HECK! I WAS AN **AWESOME** EMPRESS; THE SAVIOR OF THE ICONS, NO LESS. WHAT HAD MY **SON** EVER DONE EXCEPT SIT AROUND THE PALACE PICKING HIS NOSE!?

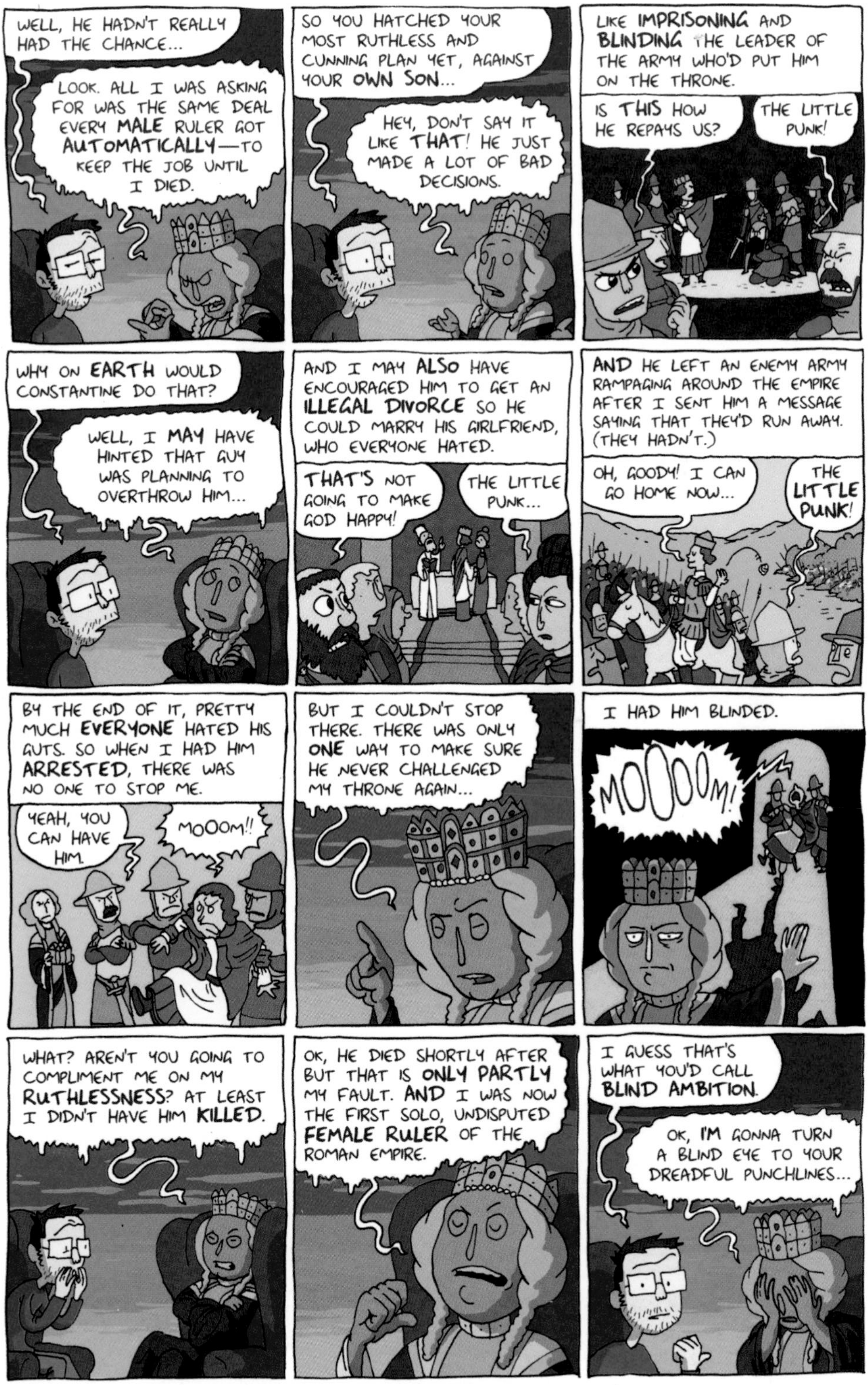
WELL, HE HADN'T REALLY HAD THE CHANCE...
LOOK. ALL I WAS ASKING FOR WAS THE SAME DEAL EVERY MALE RULER GOT AUTOMATICALLY—TO KEEP THE JOB UNTIL I DIED.
SO YOU HATCHED YOUR MOST RUTHLESS AND CUNNING PLAN YET, AGAINST YOUR OWN SON...
HEY, DON'T SAY IT LIKE THAT! HE JUST MADE A LOT OF BAD DECISIONS.
LIKE IMPRISONING AND BLINDING THE LEADER OF THE ARMY WHO'D PUT HIM ON THE THRONE.
IS THIS HOW HE REPAYS US?
THE LITTLE PUNK!
WHY ON EARTH WOULD CONSTANTINE DO THAT?
WELL, I MAY HAVE HINTED THAT GUY WAS PLANNING TO OVERTHROW HIM...
AND I MAY ALSO HAVE ENCOURAGED HIM TO GET AN ILLEGAL DIVORCE SO HE COULD MARRY HIS GIRLFRIEND, WHO EVERYONE HATED.
THAT'S NOT GOING TO MAKE GOD HAPPY!
THE LITTLE PUNK...
AND HE LEFT AN ENEMY ARMY RAMPAGING AROUND THE EMPIRE AFTER I SENT HIM A MESSAGE SAYING THAT THEY'D RUN AWAY. (THEY HADN'T.)
OH, GOODY! I CAN GO HOME NOW...
THE LITTLE PUNK!
BY THE END OF IT, PRETTY MUCH EVERYONE HATED HIS GUTS. SO WHEN I HAD HIM ARRESTED, THERE WAS NO ONE TO STOP ME.
YEAH, YOU CAN HAVE HIM.
MOOOM!!
BUT I COULDN'T STOP THERE. THERE WAS ONLY ONE WAY TO MAKE SURE HE NEVER CHALLENGED MY THRONE AGAIN...
I HAD HIM BLINDED.
MOOOOM!
WHAT? AREN'T YOU GOING TO COMPLIMENT ME ON MY RUTHLESSNESS? AT LEAST I DIDN'T HAVE HIM KILLED.
OK, HE DIED SHORTLY AFTER BUT THAT IS ONLY PARTLY MY FAULT. AND I WAS NOW THE FIRST SOLO, UNDISPUTED FEMALE RULER OF THE ROMAN EMPIRE.
I GUESS THAT'S WHAT YOU'D CALL BLIND AMBITION.
OK, I'M GONNA TURN A BLIND EYE TO YOUR DREADFUL PUNCHLINES...

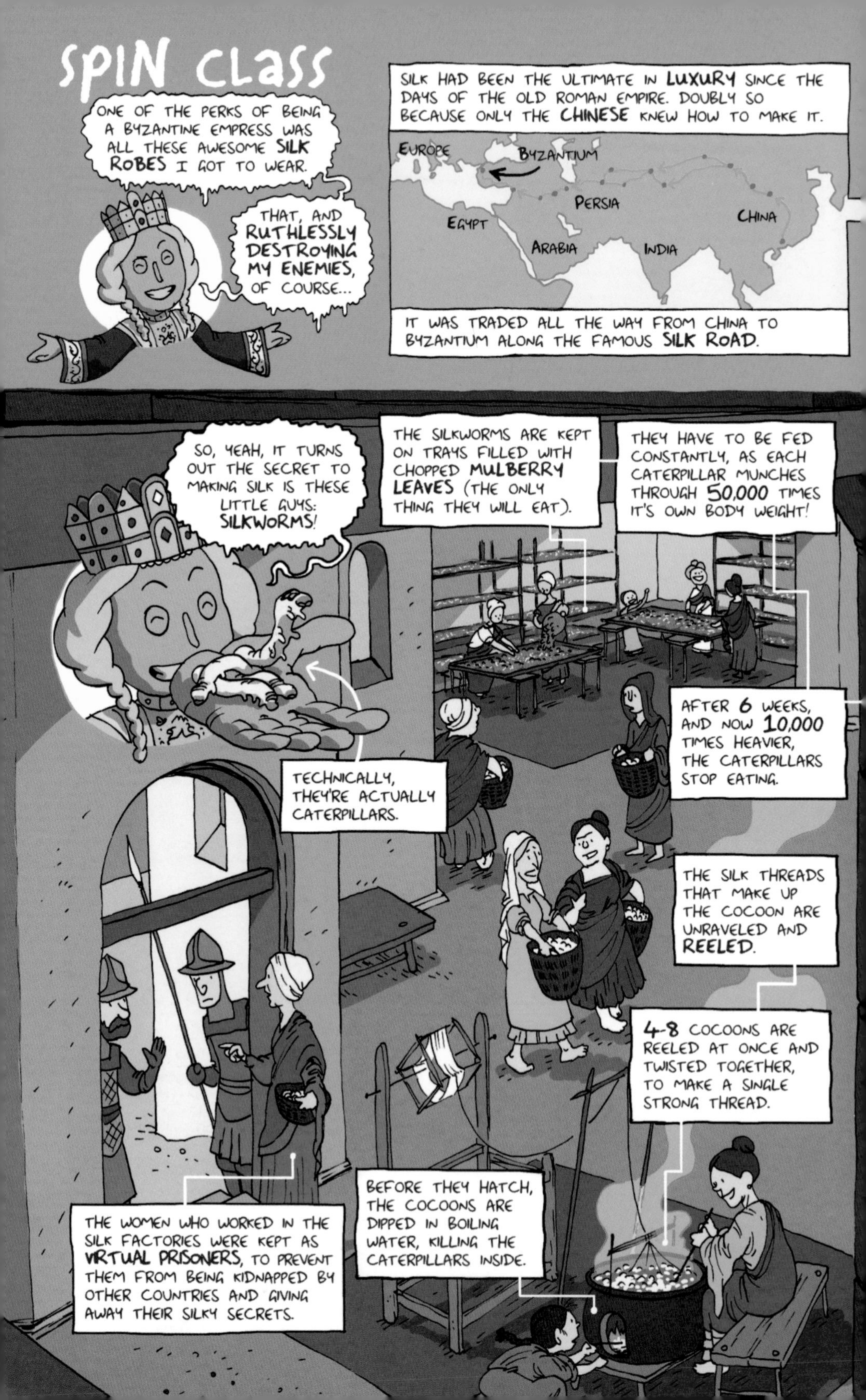
SPIN CLASS
ONE OF THE PERKS OF BEING A BYZANTINE EMPRESS WAS ALL THESE AWESOME SILK ROBES I GOT TO WEAR.
THAT, AND RUTHLESSLY DESTROYING MY ENEMIES, OF COURSE...
SILK HAD BEEN THE ULTIMATE IN LUXURY SINCE THE DAYS OF THE OLD ROMAN EMPIRE. DOUBLY SO BECAUSE ONLY THE CHINESE KNEW HOW TO MAKE IT.
EUROPE
BYZANTIUM
PERSIA
EGYPT
ARABIA
INDIA
CHINA
IT WAS TRADED ALL THE WAY FROM CHINA TO BYZANTIUM ALONG THE FAMOUS SILK ROAD.
SO, YEAH, IT TURNS OUT THE SECRET TO MAKING SILK IS THESE LITTLE GUYS: SILKWORMS!
TECHNICALLY, THEY'RE ACTUALLY CATERPILLARS.
THE SILKWORMS ARE KEPT ON TRAYS FILLED WITH CHOPPED MULBERRY LEAVES (THE ONLY THING THEY WILL EAT).
THEY HAVE TO BE FED CONSTANTLY, AS EACH CATERPILLAR MUNCHES THROUGH 50,000 TIMES IT'S OWN BODY WEIGHT!
AFTER 6 WEEKS, AND NOW 10,000 TIMES HEAVIER, THE CATERPILLARS STOP EATING.
THE SILK THREADS THAT MAKE UP THE COCOON ARE UNRAVELED AND REELED.
4-8 COCOONS ARE REELED AT ONCE AND TWISTED TOGETHER, TO MAKE A SINGLE STRONG THREAD.
BEFORE THEY HATCH, THE COCOONS ARE DIPPED IN BOILING WATER, KILLING THE CATERPILLARS INSIDE.
THE WOMEN WHO WORKED IN THE SILK FACTORIES WERE KEPT AS VIRTUAL PRISONERS, TO PREVENT THEM FROM BEING KIDNAPPED BY OTHER COUNTRIES AND GIVING AWAY THEIR SILKY SECRETS.

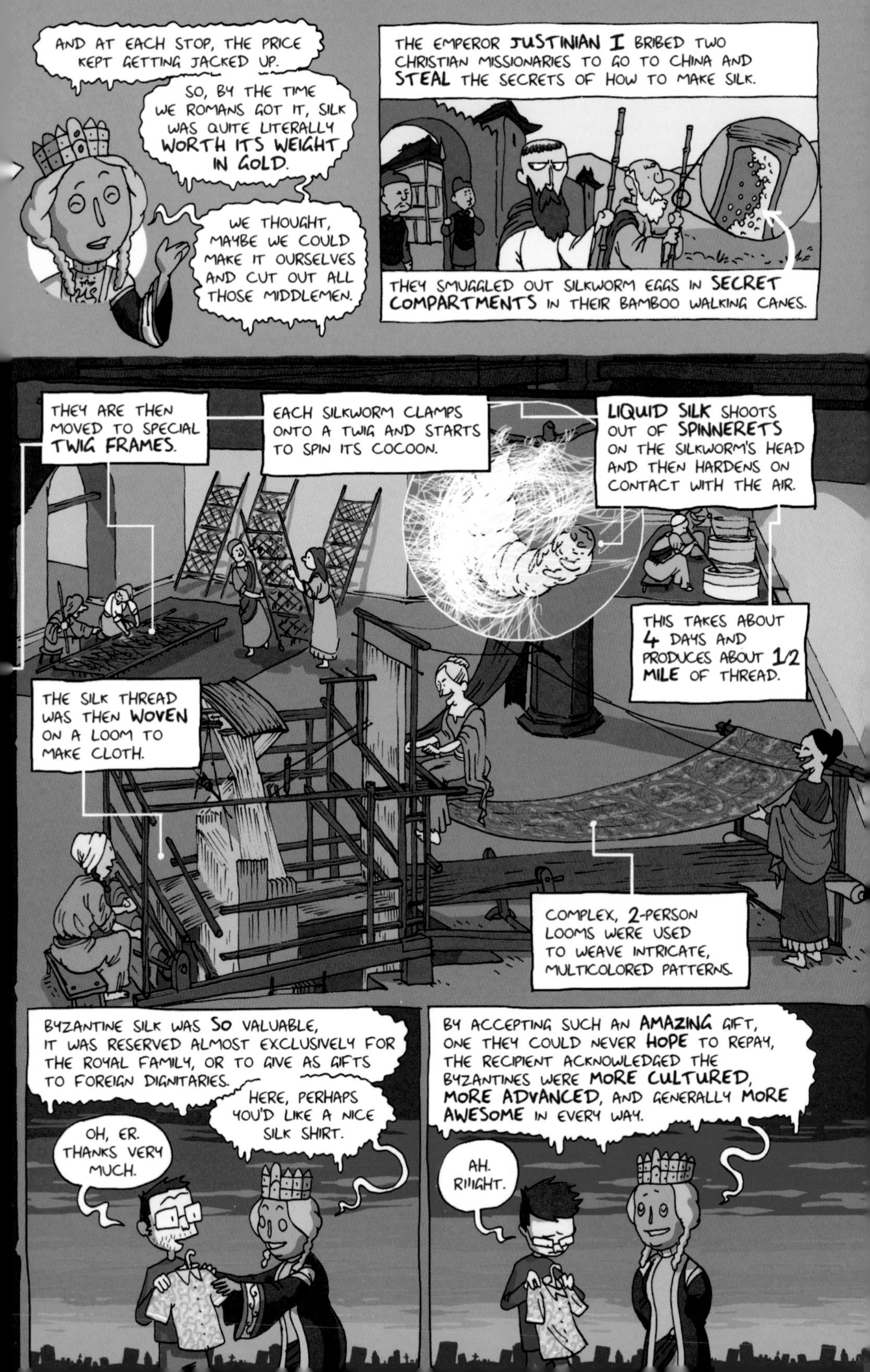
AND AT EACH STOP, THE PRICE KEPT GETTING JACKED UP.
SO, BY THE TIME WE ROMANS GOT IT, SILK WAS QUITE LITERALLY WORTH ITS WEIGHT IN GOLD.
WE THOUGHT, MAYBE WE COULD MAKE IT OURSELVES AND CUT OUT ALL THOSE MIDDLEMEN.
THE EMPEROR JUSTINIAN I BRIBED TWO CHRISTIAN MISSIONARIES TO GO TO CHINA AND STEAL THE SECRETS OF HOW TO MAKE SILK.
THEY SMUGGLED OUT SILKWORM EGGS IN SECRET COMPARTMENTS IN THEIR BAMBOO WALKING CANES.
THEY ARE THEN MOVED TO SPECIAL TWIG FRAMES.
EACH SILKWORM CLAMPS ONTO A TWIG AND STARTS TO SPIN ITS COCOON.
LIQUID SILK SHOOTS OUT OF SPINNERETS ON THE SILKWORM'S HEAD AND THEN HARDENS ON CONTACT WITH THE AIR.
THIS TAKES ABOUT 4 DAYS AND PRODUCES ABOUT 1/2 MILE OF THREAD.
THE SILK THREAD WAS THEN WOVEN ON A LOOM TO MAKE CLOTH.
COMPLEX, 2-PERSON LOOMS WERE USED TO WEAVE INTRICATE, MULTICOLORED PATTERNS.
BYZANTINE SILK WAS SO VALUABLE, IT WAS RESERVED ALMOST EXCLUSIVELY FOR THE ROYAL FAMILY, OR TO GIVE AS GIFTS TO FOREIGN DIGNITARIES.
HERE, PERHAPS YOU'D LIKE A NICE SILK SHIRT.
OH, ER. THANKS VERY MUCH.
BY ACCEPTING SUCH AN AMAZING GIFT, ONE THEY COULD NEVER HOPE TO REPAY, THE RECIPIENT ACKNOWLEDGED THE BYZANTINES WERE MORE CULTURED, MORE ADVANCED, AND GENERALLY MORE AWESOME IN EVERY WAY.
AH. RIIIGHT.

PLEASE WELCOME MY NEXT GUEST! SHE'S A **FOOL-FLINGING**, **SUITOR-SMACKDOWNING**, **WRESTLEMANIA-INDUCING** **WARRIOR WOMAN**...

GET READY FOR A **ROYAL RUMBLE** WITH MONGOLIA'S WRESTLING PRINCESS...

# KHUTULUN!

KHUTULUN
WRESTLING PRINCESS
💀 1260s—1300s 💀

KHUTULUN, DESPITE BEING THE DAUGHTER OF THE GREAT KHAN **QAIDU**, YOU GREW UP PRETTY **HARDCORE** IN THE TRADITIONAL **MONGOL** LIFESTYLE.

YEAH, WELL, WE WERE **NOMADS**, WHICH MEANS WE MOVED AROUND ALL THE TIME TO FIND FRESH GRAZING LAND FOR OUR HERDS.

WE MEASURED WEALTH NOT IN GOLD AND JEWELS, BUT IN **HORSES**, WHICH ARE **MUCH** MORE USEFUL SINCE YOU CAN RIDE 'EM, DRINK THEIR MILK, AND EVEN **EAT** 'EM IF YOU HAVE TO.

LIKE ALL MONGOL KIDS, I LEARNED TO RIDE AND SHOOT AS SOON AS I COULD WALK.

AND IT'S ALL THAT **PRACTICE** THAT MADE US THE UNBEATABLE FIGHTING FORCE THAT'D CONQUERED MOST OF THE KNOWN WORLD UNDER MY GREAT-GRANDPA, **GENGHIS KHAN.**

OUR MONGOL ARCHERS WERE FAMOUS FOR BEING ABLE TO SHOOT **BIRDS IN FLIGHT** OUT OF THE SKY.

*SQUAK!*

**WHILE RIDING,** I MIGHT ADD, WE LEARNED TO WAIT FOR THE EXACT MOMENT WHEN ALL **4** HORSE HOOVES WERE OFF THE GROUND TO SHOOT.

WE WERE **ALSO** FAMOUS FOR TRICKS LIKE SLIDING DOWN THE **SIDE** OF OUR HORSE AND SHOOTING FROM UNDERNEATH.

OK, THAT'S JUST SHOWING OFF NOW...

I WAS, FRANKLY, PRETTY EXCEPTIONAL AT ALL OF THESE THINGS, BUT MY REAL PASSION WAS ALWAYS **WRESTLING!**

GROWING UP AS THE YOUNGEST, AND THE ONLY SISTER OF **14** BROTHERS, I GOT PLENTY OF LESSONS IN THE WRESTLING SCHOOL OF **HARD KNOCKS.**

MAYBE THAT'S PART OF THE REASON I GOT SO **GOOD.**

BUT ALL OF THESE TRADITIONAL MONGOL PASTIMES WERE REALLY JUST TRAINING FOR THE **MOST** TRADITIONAL, MOST **MONGOL-EST** PASTIME OF ALL: SMITING OUR ENEMIES...

AND I FOUND A WAY TO COMBINE THEM ALL! I'D RIDE ALONG THE FRONT OF THE ENEMY ARMY USING MY MONGOL SUPER-SOLDIER SKILLS TO DODGE THEIR SPEARS AND ARROWS...

THEN I'D **GRAB** SOME POOR CHUMP, **WRESTLE** HIM OFF HIS HORSE, AND DRAG HIM BACK TO MY DAD FOR A BIT OF **SMITING** ACTION.

HAR, HAR! SCARED THE LIVING DAYLIGHTS OUT OF 'EM!

WHAT JUST HAPPENED?

WAS THAT A GIRL?

WHERE'D CHEN GO?

WITH YOUR EXTRAORDINARY COMBAT CAPABILITIES, YOU BECAME YOUR DAD'S **CHIEF MILITARY ADVISER.**

YOUR **14** OLDER BROTHERS MUST'VE **LOVED** THAT...

UPSTAGED BY A GIRL!

ARR. WE'LL SHOW HER...

YEAH, THEY WEREN'T THRILLED. BUT MONGOL SOCIETY **DID SOMETIMES** ALLOW WOMEN TO HOLD POSITIONS OF POWER THAT WOULD'VE BEEN **UNTHINKABLE** IN THE SO-CALLED "CIVILIZED WORLD."

WHAT WITH ALL THE RIDING, SHOOTING AND WRESTLING WE WERE ALREADY DOING, IT WASN'T UNCOMMON FOR WOMEN TO JOIN THE ARMY.

AND EVEN THE GREAT **GENGHIS KHAN** HIMSELF PUT HIS DAUGHTERS IN CHARGE OF KEY TERRITORIES HE DIDN'T TRUST HIS SONS WITH.

DID I MENTION HE'S MY GREAT-GRANDPA?

BUT WOMEN STILL HAD TO MARRY WHOMEVER THEIR FATHER **TOLD** THEM TO.

OK, I KNOW, I KNOW, BUT HIS DAD'S **VERY** RICH...

THINK OF ALL THOSE **HORSES**...

I'M SURE I DON'T NEED TO EXPLAIN HOW **ROTTEN** IT IS TO BE MARRIED TO A MAN YOU DON'T LOVE, DON'T EVEN **LIKE**, AND WHO TREATS YOU LIKE **DIRT**.

SO I CAME UP WITH A CUNNING PLAN...

I'LL ONLY MARRY THE MAN WHO CAN **BEAT** ME AT WRESTLING!

IT WAS PERFECT—**I** KNEW I WAS UNBEATABLE, SO I DIDN'T HAVE TO WORRY ABOUT LOSING...

AND, OF COURSE, IT WORKED WELL ON ALL THESE MACHO MONGOL MALES...

GRR! YOU **CAN'T** GET BEATEN BY A **GIRL**!

DO IT! OR YOU'LL LOOK LIKE A WIMP!

BOOM!

NATURALLY, THE DOWNSIDE WAS THAT EVERYONE HEARD THEY COULD MARRY A **PRINCESS** JUST BY WINNING A WRESTLING MATCH. I HAD TO START MAKING THEM WAGER **100** HORSES A POP, JUST TO WEED OUT ALL THE TIME-WASTERS...

BY THE END OF IT, I HAD AN UNBEATEN RECORD AND A HERD OF OVER **10,000** HORSES!

**AND** I GOT MARRIED WHEN **I** CHOSE, TO A GUY I WAS ACTUALLY IN LOVE WITH.

ALL **RIGHT!** NOW **THAT'S** WHAT I CALL A TRIPLE-SUPLEX TOP-ROPE **BODY SLAM** OF A HAPPY ENDING!

ACTUALLY, THE STORY'S NOT QUITE DONE YET...

BEFORE DAD DIED, HE NAMED **ME** AS THE NEXT KHAN!

GEEZ. YOUR BROTHERS MUST'VE **REALLY** LOVED THAT...

-SIGH- IT WAS A **TOTAL** HASSLE...

YOU SEE, THE KHAN WASN'T **REALLY** LIKE A KING OR QUEEN— YOU DIDN'T GET THE JOB **JUST** BASED ON WHO YOUR DAD WAS. THE WHOLE GENGHIS FAMILY HAD TO AGREE ON IT.

WELL, **I** THINK SHE'D MAKE A SPLENDID KHAN...

OH, YEAH? WELL **I** THINK YOU SHOULD BUTT OUT, OLD LADY...

WELL, **I** THINK **YOU** NEED A LESSON IN MANNERS...

MONGOL-STYLE...

I DIDN'T EVEN **WANT** TO BE KHAN! TOO MUCH PAPERWORK, NOT ENOUGH ACTION...

PLUS, THE CONSTANT, LINGERING THREAT OF ASSASSINATION...

SO I BACKED THE **LEAST STUPID** OF MY BROTHERS FOR THE JOB, AND IN RETURN GOT TO KEEP MY POSITION AS CHIEF MILITARY ADVISER.

LEAVING YOU FREE TO DO WHAT YOU DO BEST— SMITING YOUR ENEMIES AND BODYSLAMMING FOOLS INTO THE DIRT.

WELL, I THINK EVERYONE SHOULD FOLLOW THEIR CALLING...

# MONGOLIAN MOVES!

I'VE ASKED **KHUTULUN**, THE WRESTLING PRINCESS, TO TELL US A BIT MORE ABOUT HER SPORT: THE MONGOLIAN WRESTLING STYLE KNOWN AS **BÖKH**.

AW, YEAH!

IT WAS ACTUALLY MY GREAT-GRANDAD, **GENGHIS KHAN**, WHO GOT THE MONGOLS HOOKED ON WRESTLING, TO KEEP THEM IN SHAPE FOR CONQUERING THE WORLD.

THE RULES ARE PRETTY SIMPLE:

- NO HITTING, STRANGLING, EYE-POKING, OR BEING RUDE.

- NO TIME LIMIT. TAKE AS LONG AS YOU LIKE!

- NO RING. USE AS MUCH SPACE AS YOU LIKE!

- FIRST TO TOUCH THE GROUND LOSES (ANY PART OF THE BODY ABOVE THE FEET)

SIMPLE RULES, BUT BÖKH IS ACTUALLY FULL OF SUBTLE TACTICS FOR CATCHING YOUR OPPONENT OFF-BALANCE. THERE ARE TWO MAIN STRATEGIES:

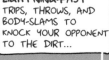

**LIGHTNING-FAST** TRIPS, THROWS, AND BODY-SLAMS TO KNOCK YOUR OPPONENT TO THE DIRT...

OR SLOWLY WEARING THEM DOWN IN A GRUELING BATTLE OF ENDURANCE, PATIENCE, AND **WILL**...

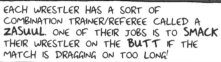

EACH WRESTLER HAS A SORT OF COMBINATION TRAINER/REFEREE CALLED A **ZASUUL**. ONE OF THEIR JOBS IS TO **SMACK** THEIR WRESTLER ON THE **BUTT** IF THE MATCH IS DRAGGING ON TOO LONG!

SINCE THERE'S NO TIME LIMIT, MATCHES CAN GO ON FOR **HOURS**!

BÖKH TOURNAMENTS BEGIN WITH THE WRESTLERS PERFORMING THEIR TRADITIONAL **EAGLE DANCE**, WHICH CALLS DOWN THE SPIRIT OF THAT MAJESTIC BIRD TO INSPIRE THEIR WRESTLING. AND IT'S A NICE WARM-UP, TOO.

UM, CAN I JUST ASK... WHAT'S THE DEAL WITH THESE LITTLE JACKET THINGIES THEY'RE WEARING?

THAT'S THE TRADITIONAL BÖKH WRESTLING OUTFIT.

LEGEND TELLS OF AN -AHEM- MIGHTY WRESTLING PRINCESS WHO WENT AROUND BEATING ALL THE MEN **SO BADLY** THEY SWORE NEVER TO LET ANOTHER WOMAN COMPETE.

THE JACKET LETS THEM CHECK...

OK, DEFINITELY NOT A GIRL...

SO, THERE'S NO WOMEN'S WRESTLING ANY MORE!?

NOT AT THE **NAADAM**, THE OFFICIAL MONGOLIAN BÖKH TOURNAMENT. BUT THINGS ARE CHANGING...

MONGOLIAN WOMEN WRESTLERS HAVE BECOME **NATIONAL CELEBRITIES** AFTER TAKING HOME MEDALS IN BOTH THE OLYMPICS AND THE WORLD WRESTLING CHAMPIONSHIPS.

AND THEY'RE INSPIRING THE **NEXT** GENERATION OF GIRL WRESTLERS WITH THE WARRIOR SPIRIT OF **KHUTULUN!**

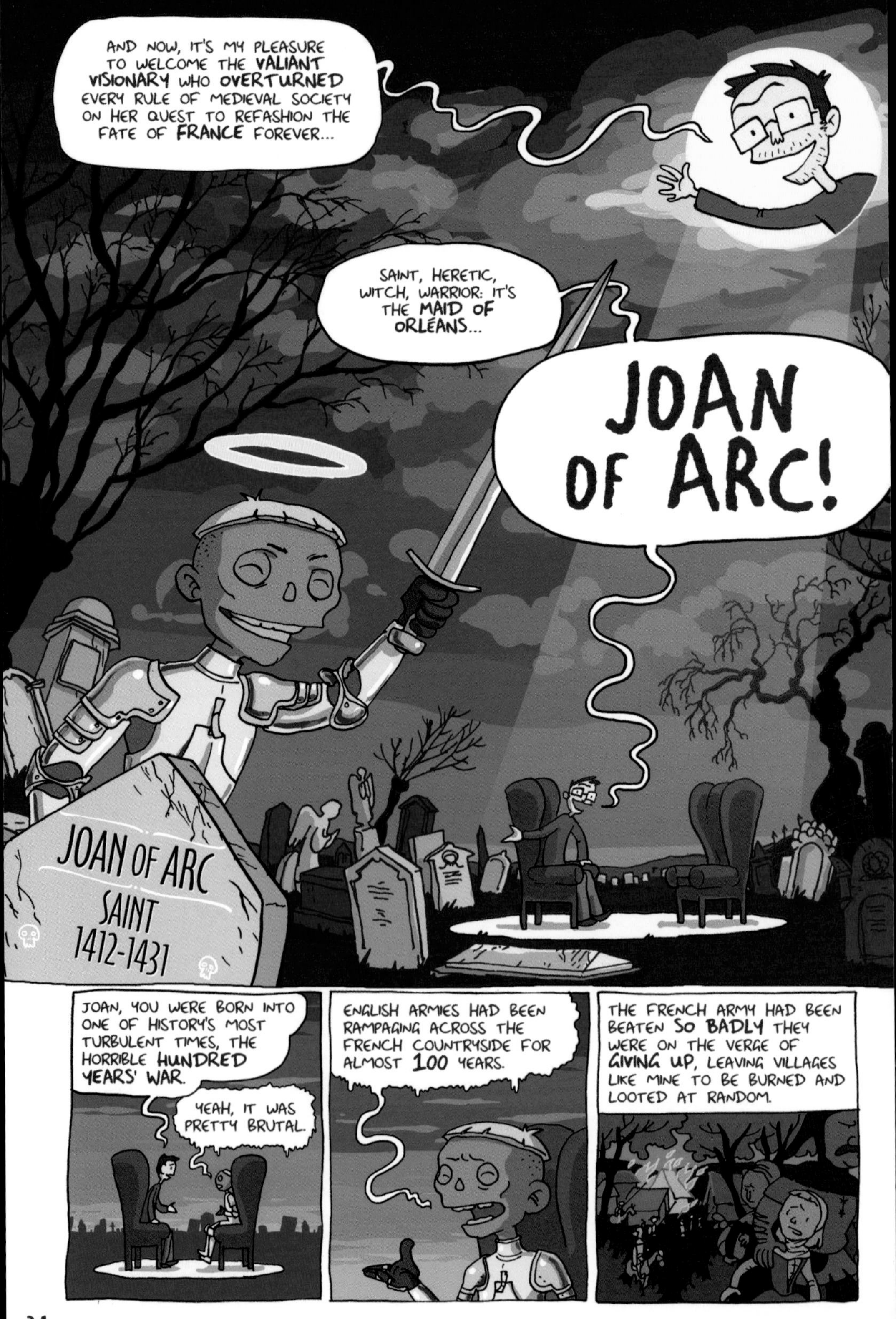

AND NOW, IT'S MY PLEASURE TO WELCOME THE **VALIANT VISIONARY** WHO **OVERTURNED** EVERY RULE OF MEDIEVAL SOCIETY ON HER QUEST TO REFASHION THE FATE OF **FRANCE** FOREVER...
SAINT, HERETIC, WITCH, WARRIOR: IT'S THE **MAID OF ORLÉANS**...
JOAN OF ARC!
JOAN OF ARC
SAINT
1412-1431
JOAN, YOU WERE BORN INTO ONE OF HISTORY'S MOST TURBULENT TIMES, THE HORRIBLE **HUNDRED YEARS' WAR**.
YEAH, IT WAS PRETTY BRUTAL.
ENGLISH ARMIES HAD BEEN RAMPAGING ACROSS THE FRENCH COUNTRYSIDE FOR ALMOST **100** YEARS.
THE FRENCH ARMY HAD BEEN BEATEN **SO BADLY** THEY WERE ON THE VERGE OF **GIVING UP**, LEAVING VILLAGES LIKE MINE TO BE BURNED AND LOOTED AT RANDOM.

SO YOU DECIDED, IF NO ONE ELSE WAS GOING TO DO SOMETHING ABOUT IT, **YOU WOULD!**

OH, **I** DIDN'T DECIDE IT—THE **VOICES** DID.

MICHAEL THE ARCHANGEL AND SAINTS CATHERINE AND MARGARET CAME TO ME IN A SHINING LIGHT AND TOLD ME **I** WAS THE ONE WHO WOULD SAVE FRANCE.

UM, RIGHT, SO THESE... UH... VOICES... ARE YOU SURE THEY WEREN'T JUST IN YOUR **IMAGINATION?**

SURE—WHY NOT? THAT'S JUST HOW THE MESSAGES OF GOD COME TO US.

AND GOD WAS TELLING ME TO CUT MY HAIR, RIDE TO THE KING OF FRANCE, AND SAVE HIS KINGDOM.

MY KING. **GOD** HAS SENT ME.

OH, THAT'S FAB.

WHAT DID THE KING MAKE OF YOUR... ER... VOICES?

OH, HE WAS A BIG FAN.

PLUS, HIS PEOPLE WERE SO DEMORALIZED BY DEFEAT, THEY WERE ACTUALLY WELCOMING THE ENGLISH...

NO, REALLY. PLEASE TAKE OVER. OUR KING'S A LOSER, ANYWAY...

HE PROBABLY FIGURED A LITTLE **MORAL SUPPORT** FROM **GOD** WOULDN'T GO AMISS.

SO HE GAVE YOU A CUSTOM-MADE SUIT OF ARMOR AND SENT YOU OFF AT THE HEAD OF AN ARMY TO SAVE THE ABOUT-TO-SURRENDER CITY OF **ORLÉANS.**

RIGHT! THE FIRST THING I DID WAS TO REMIND THE ARMY THAT THEY WERE FIGHTING ON **GOD'S** SIDE. WHICH IS WHY I MADE THEM ALL GIVE UP SWEARING...

...AND THEY ALL HAD TO GO TO CHURCH AND CONFESS THEIR SINS.

...SO THEN I KICKED A PUPPY. AND STOLE ITS BONE. IT WAS A REALLY CUTE PUPPY, TOO...

AND WHEN THEY WENT INTO BATTLE I WAS RIGHT THERE AT THEIR HEAD, CHEERING THEM ON AND PRAYING LIKE CRAZY.

THEN YOU DIDN'T ACTUALLY, Y'KNOW, KILL ANYONE? YOU WERE MORE OF A SORT OF **HOLY CHEERLEADER**?

BAH! THAT'S WHAT THE OLD ARMY GENERALS THOUGHT.

BASICALLY, THEY WANTED TO IGNORE ME AND KEEP ON FIGHTING SLOW, CAREFUL, BY-THE-BOOK WARFARE.

OK, RUN ALONG LITTLE GIRL—THIS ISN'T A GAME.

BUT I WASN'T GOING TO BE IGNORED!

WHAT'S **WRONG** WITH YOU! YOU'VE GOT **GOD** ON YOUR SIDE—YOU CAN'T LOSE! QUIT FARTING AROUND!

UH, THAT'S A SWEAR...

AND YOUR COMBINATION OF **HOLY PURITY** AND **STORM-THE-WALLS AGGRESSION** PROVED TO BE JUST WHAT WAS NEEDED TO TURN AN ARMY OF LOSERS BACK INTO FIGHTING FRENCHMEN!

YOU LIBERATED ORLÉANS IN RECORD TIME, AND THEN PUSHED ON, DEEP INTO ENEMY TERRITORY, TO THE CATHEDRAL CITY OF **REIMS.**

English channel

Reims

Rouen

English territory

Paris

OW!

Joan's march

Orléans

OOF!

Chinon (King)

French territory

REIMS WAS THE ONLY PLACE WHERE THE TRUE KING OF FRANCE COULD BE CROWNED. NOW NO ONE WOULD THINK HE WAS A LOSER EVER AGAIN! THE KINGDOM WAS SAVED!

MISSION ACCOMPLISHED! YAY! SO YOU COULD GO HOME, RIGHT?

UH, NOT QUITE.

THE ENGLISH WERE STILL IN FRANCE. BUT NOW THE KING WAS SECURE ON HIS THRONE, HE STOPPED FIGHTING AND STARTED **NEGOTIATING** WITH THEM...

HE WAS SO EAGER TO MAKE NICE, HE WAS GIVING TOWNS BACK TO THE ENGLISH AND THEIR ALLIES!

IT'S CALLED DIPLOMACY, JOAN—LOOK IT UP...

WELL, THAT WAS THE LAST STRAW! I GRABBED WHOEVER WOULD STILL FOLLOW ME AND MARCHED OFF TO SAVE THOSE TOWNS!

BUT WITHOUT THE KING'S SUPPORT, YOU WERE QUICKLY OUTNUMBERED, OVERWHELMED, AND CAPTURED.

AND THE ENGLISH WEREN'T GOING TO BE HAPPY WITH A SIMPLE EXECUTION...

SHE'S MADE **US** LOOK LIKE THE **BAD GUYS!**

THEY PLANNED TO IMPROVE THEIR P.R. IMAGE BY... KILLING YOU...?

WELL, THEY WANTED TO QUASH THE BELIEF THAT **GOD** WANTED THEM OUT OF FRANCE!

SO THEY SET UP A TOTALLY BOGUS **SHAM TRIAL** TO PROVE MY VISIONS WERE REALLY SENT BY **THE DEVIL!**

WAIT—IF THEY JUST WANTED TO DISPROVE THE **VISIONS**... COULD YOU NOT JUST SAY YOU **MADE IT ALL UP!?**

I DID, GOD FORGIVE ME! WHEN THEY TOOK ME DOWN TO THE EXECUTION SQUARE AND I FELT THE HEAT OF THE FIRE, I LIED AND SAID I'D INVENTED THE WHOLE THING.

BUT I COULDN'T GO THROUGH WITH IT! MY VISIONS WERE GOOD AND TRUE! BETTER TO DIE FOR THE TRUTH THAN TO LIVE A LIE!

AND SO ON MAY **30, 1431,** YOU WERE BURNED ALIVE AND YOUR ASHES WERE SCATTERED ON THE SEINE RIVER.

I CAN'T EVEN IMAGINE! THE PAIN, THE HEAT, THE...

HOLD ON...

IF YOU WERE **BURNED TO ASHES**...

HOW CAN YOU BE **HERE?**

OH, BUT AM I?

OR IS THIS ALL JUST IN YOUR **IMAGINATION**...?

JOAN OF ARC WAS BURNED AS A **HERETIC**. BUT THE CHURCH LATER CHANGED ITS MIND, EVENTUALLY EVEN MAKING HER A **SAINT**!

HA! HOW D'YOU LIKE ME **NOW**, INQUISITORIAL COURT OF ROUEN, **1431**?

BUT, SERIOUSLY THOUGH, THAT'S NOT QUITE RIGHT. THE CHURCH DOESN'T **MAKE** SAINTS. TECHNICALLY, **ANYONE** IN HEAVEN IS A SAINT **ALREADY**.

THE CHURCH CERTIFIES THAT SOME PEOPLE ARE **DEFINITELY** SAINTS.

SO... **HOW DO YOU BECOME A**

## STEP 2: GATHER A FLOCK

A SAINT-IN-THE-MAKING WILL OFTEN HAVE A BIT OF A FAN CLUB AMONG PEOPLE WHO KNEW THEM OR WHO COME FROM THE SAME AREA.

IF ENOUGH PEOPLE START PRAYING TO THEM, THE LOCAL **BISHOP** WILL WRITE UP A REPORT ON WHY THEY'D MAKE A GOOD SAINT, AND SEND IT TO THE HEAD OF THE **CATHOLIC CHURCH**—THE POPE.

DON'T FORGET THE TIME SHE HELPED ME FIND THAT QUARTER IN THE COUCH CUSHIONS.

## STEP 4: WORK SOME MIRACLES

THE THEORY IS: IF YOU ARE IN HEAVEN, YOU CAN BEND **GOD'S** EAR TO HELP SOMEONE OUT. SO A MIRACLE **PROVES** YOU ARE A SAINT.

CAN WE SPRING FOR THE BIKE, TOO...?

FOR A MIRACULOUS **HEALING**, A PANEL OF **INDEPENDENT DOCTORS** MUST DECLARE THAT THEY CAN'T FIND A KNOWN **MEDICAL** REASON FOR A CURE.

I FEEL GREAT!

HALLELUJAH!

I HAD TO WORK **4** MIRACLES AT THIS STAGE.

**SAVING FRANCE** COUNTS AS ONE, AND THEN **3** FRENCH NUNS GOT MIRACULOUSLY CURED BY PRAYING TO ME. BOOM!

BUT EVEN THAT'S NOT ENOUGH. YOU STILL HAVE TO...

NOWADAYS, THE PROCESS OF ACHIEVING SAINTHOOD IS PRETTY STRICT. **POPE FRANCIS** INTRODUCED NEW, TOUGHER RULES FOR ESTABLISHING MIRACLES, FOR EXAMPLE.

BUT IN THE PAST, IT OFTEN CAME DOWN TO JUST HAVING AN **AWESOME STORY**—LIKE...

### ST. QUITERIA

LED A NONUPLET, JAILBREAKING GIRL GANG.

### ST. DENIS

WALKED **7** MILES WITH HIS HEAD CUT OFF.

**STEP 1: GO TO HEAVEN!**

YOU CAN'T BE IN HEAVEN IF YOU'RE STILL **ALIVE**. I MEAN, **OBVIOUSLY**.

YOU ALSO HAVE TO WAIT AT LEAST **5** YEARS FOR THE EMOTIONS AROUND YOUR DEATH TO CALM DOWN.

**I** HAD TO WAIT EVEN LONGER—I DIDN'T BECOME AN OFFICIAL SAINT UNTIL **1920**. THAT'S ALMOST **500** YEARS LATER!

GEEZ, LOUISE. WHAT'S THE HOLD UP...?

**STEP 3: GET THE POPE'S SEAL OF APPROVAL**

THE POPE'S SAINT-CERTIFYING **TASK FORCE** DOES ITS OWN INVESTIGATION.

WAS THIS PROSPECTIVE SAINT **REALLY** AS SAINTLY AS EVERYONE SAYS? OR DO THEY HAVE A FEW **SINFUL SKELETONS** HIDING IN THEIR CLOSET?

WELL, I HEARD SHE ATTACKED PARIS ON THE VIRGIN MARY'S **BIRTHDAY**...

HMM...

COME ON! ARE YOU KIDDING ME!?

**STEP 5: WORK MORE MIRACLES!**

YUP, THE CHURCH REALLY WANTS TO SEE THOSE MIRACLES! AND THESE ONES HAVE TO HAPPEN **AFTER** YOU'VE ALREADY PASSED STEP **4**.

I CURED **2 MORE** NUNS— ONE WITH TUBERCULOSIS AND ONE WITH A **HOLE IN THE FOOT** (YES, REALLY).

NEED A **HOLE-Y** MIRACLE HERE. PLEASE, JOAN...

BOOM AND BOOM! THAT'S PRETTY INCONTROVERTIBLE. AND A **SAINT IS BORN!**

**ST. SIMEON THE STYLITE**

LIVED ON TOP OF A **50**FT PILLAR IN THE **DESERT**.

**ST. MARGARET OF ANTIOCH**

**BUSTED OUT** OF A DRAGON'S STOMACH USING A CROSS.

WOW, I NEVER KNEW THERE WERE SO MANY ROUTES TO SAINTHOOD!

NOW I JUST NEED TO FIND A **DRAGON**...

MAYBE THERE'S HOPE FOR YOU YET...

AND NOW, I'D LIKE YOU TO WELCOME ONE OF HISTORY'S MOST FAMOUS **FIGHTING FEMALES!** IT'S NONE OTHER THAN THE MONARCH SUPREME...

...THE LEAN, MEAN TUDOR QUEEN...

ELIZABETH I !

ELIZABETH I
QUEEN OF ENGLAND
1533-1603

ELIZABETH, YOU MIGHT BE THE WORLD-RECORD HOLDER FOR THE MOST **IINSANE** FAMILY DRAMA **OF ALL TIME!**

YOUR FATHER, **HENRY VIII,** WAS SO DESPERATE TO HAVE A SON AND HEIR THAT HE MADE UP A **WHOLE NEW CHURCH,** JUST SO HE COULD DIVORCE HIS WIFE AND MARRY YOUR MOTHER, **ANNE BOLEYN!**

BUT AFTER **YOU** WERE BORN, HE GREW SO ANGRY THAT ANNE HADN'T GIVEN BIRTH TO A BOY THAT HE HAD HER **DECAPITATED!**

TALK ABOUT **LOSING YOUR HEAD**...

THAT'S MY **PARENTS** YOU'RE TALKING ABOUT...

WIFE NUMBER **3** GAVE HENRY HIS LONGED-FOR SON, BUT **HE** ONLY SURVIVED TO AGE **15**, LEAVING THE THRONE TO YOUR OLDER SISTER, MARY. BETTER KNOWN AS **BLOODY MARY**.

YIKES!

SHE WAS DETERMINED TO MAKE EVERYONE GIVE UP MY FATHER'S NEW CHURCH OF ENGLAND.

USING THAT TRIED-AND-TRUE METHOD OF PERSUASION, **BURNING AT THE STAKE!**

THEY'LL THANK ME WHEN THEY GET TO HEAVEN...

BUT VIOLENT ILLNESS BROUGHT AN END TO HER REIGN OF TERROR, LEAVING **ME** AS QUEEN!

YESS!

I MEAN... VERY WELL, IF GOD WILLS IT...

SUDDENLY, SEEMS LIKE EVERY GUY IN **EUROPE** WAS OUT TO MARRY YOU! PRETTY SWEET!

OBVIOUSLY, **YOU HAVEN'T SEEN THEM**...

KING PHILIP II OF SPAIN (MY DEAD SISTER'S HUSBAND. EW.)

DUKE FRANCIS OF ANJOU (LOOKS LIKE A FROG.)

PRINCE ERIK OF SWEDEN (WENT MAD AND WAS POISONED BY HIS SUBJECTS.)

WHAT A BUNCH OF LOSERS! BUT I ONLY EVER HAD EYES FOR **ONE** MAN...

ROBERT DUDLEY!

YOUR MAJESTY! YOUR HUSBAND SHOULD BE SOMEONE WHO'LL MAKE A GREAT KING.

AND WHO'S ALREADY RICH AND POWERFUL.

AND **CERTAINLY** NOT THAT **BUM** DUDLEY!

MY LORDS. I **ALWAYS** APPRECIATE YOUR ADVICE, BUT THIS IS SOMETHING A WOMAN MUST DECIDE FOR HERSELF...

SMOOTH... BUT THERE WAS **ANOTHER** REASON YOU COULDN'T MARRY **STUDLEY DUDLEY**...

YEAH, HE WAS **ALREADY** MARRIED.

THAT'S... KIND OF A PROBLEM...

BUT HIS WIFE WAS REALLY ILL...

SO YOU WERE BASICALLY **WAITING** FOR HER TO DIE?

**NO!** WELL... YEAH, KIND OF...

BUT THEN, ONE DAY SHE WAS FOUND AT THE BOTTOM OF THE STAIRS, HER NECK BROKEN...

UH OH...

**CONVENIENT!**

NO! IT WAS THE **WORST** THING THAT COULD'VE HAPPENED!

EVERYONE ASSUMED POOR ROBERT HAD KILLED HER SO HE COULD MARRY ME!

AND HE DIDN'T...?

OF **COURSE** HE DIDN'T! HE WASN'T A **TOTAL** IDIOT!

HE KNEW AS WELL AS I DID THAT I COULDN'T REMAIN QUEEN WITH THAT SORT OF SCANDAL.

MY COUSIN, MARY QUEEN OF SCOTS, MADE THAT MISTAKE. SHE MARRIED A GUY WHO HAD JUST **BLOWN UP** HER HUSBAND!

**BOOM!**

OK, GOOD TO GO...

SHE GOT KICKED OUT OF SCOTLAND OVER IT, SO SHE CAME TO ENGLAND, HOPING TO GET RID OF ME AND BECOME QUEEN IN MY PLACE...

SCOTLAND
ENGLAND

SO YOU GOT RID OF HER FIRST!

HEY! I WORKED MY **BUNS** OFF TRYING TO KEEP HER ALIVE!

BUT MY SPYMASTER CAUGHT HER WRITING SECRET LETTERS PLOTTING MY DEATH! EVEN **I** COULDN'T SAVE HER AFTER THAT!

ALL RIGHT, SO LET'S SEE... YOUR DAD KILLED YOUR MOM. YOUR SISTER'S A PSYCHO. YOUR BOYFRIEND **DIDN'T** KILL HIS WIFE, BUT EVERYONE THOUGHT HE DID. YOU COUSIN TRIED TO KILL YOU, BUT YOU GOT HER FIRST...

ALSO, DON'T FORGET MY BROTHER-IN-LAW...

HUH?

PHILIP II OF SPAIN... THE GUY WHO TRIED TO MARRY ME AFTER MY SISTER DIED.

PHIL DIDN'T TAKE **REJECTION** TOO WELL...

THAT ELIZABETH... I'LL GET HER FOR THIS...

BROOD!!

SO HE ASSEMBLED AN ENORMOUS FLEET OF SHIPS, **THE SPANISH ARMADA**, DETERMINED TO INVADE ENGLAND AND KICK ME OFF THE THRONE!

BRING IT!

FIRST WE BLASTED THEM WITH **CANNONS**!

THEN WE SAILED **SHIPS OF FIRE** INTO THEM!

THEN **GOD** GOT IN ON THE ACTION AND **STORMED THEM TO DEATH**!

SO THE MORAL OF THE STORY IS...

DON'T MESS WITH THE **BESS**!

AW, YEAH!

# A KILLER LOOK!

ELIZABETH KNEW THE IMPORTANCE OF **POWER DRESSING**—HER ENTIRE LOOK WAS DESIGNED TO STRIKE FEAR AND AWE INTO THE HEARTS OF HER SUBJECTS.

SHE BEGAN PAINTING HER FACE WITH THICK WHITE MAKEUP TO COVER THE SCARS LEFT BY THE DEADLY DISEASE **SMALLPOX**. BUT WHAT SHE DIDN'T KNOW WAS THAT **WHITE LEAD**, THE MAKEUP'S ESSENTIAL INGREDIENT, IS A **DEADLY POISON**! IN FACT, THIS MIGHT WELL BE WHAT KILLED HER.

WHITE LEAD ALSO MADE HER **BALD**: IN LATER LIFE, SHE WORE MORE AND MORE ELABORATE **WIGS**.

GOSSAMER "FAIRY WINGS" WERE A KEY PART OF THE LOOK, TO MAKE HER SEEM MAGICAL AND OTHERWORLDY.

THIS FAMOUS DRESS WAS EMBROIDERED WITH THE ANIMALS AND PLANTS OF HER KINGDOM, AND ALSO SOME **SEA MONSTERS**, TO SHOW SHE RULED THE WAVES AS WELL.

EXPENSIVE SILK, BROUGHT ALL THE WAY FROM CHINA, HIGHLIGHTED THE **PEERLESS POWER** OF THE ELIZABETHAN ENGLISH **TRADING** NETWORKS.

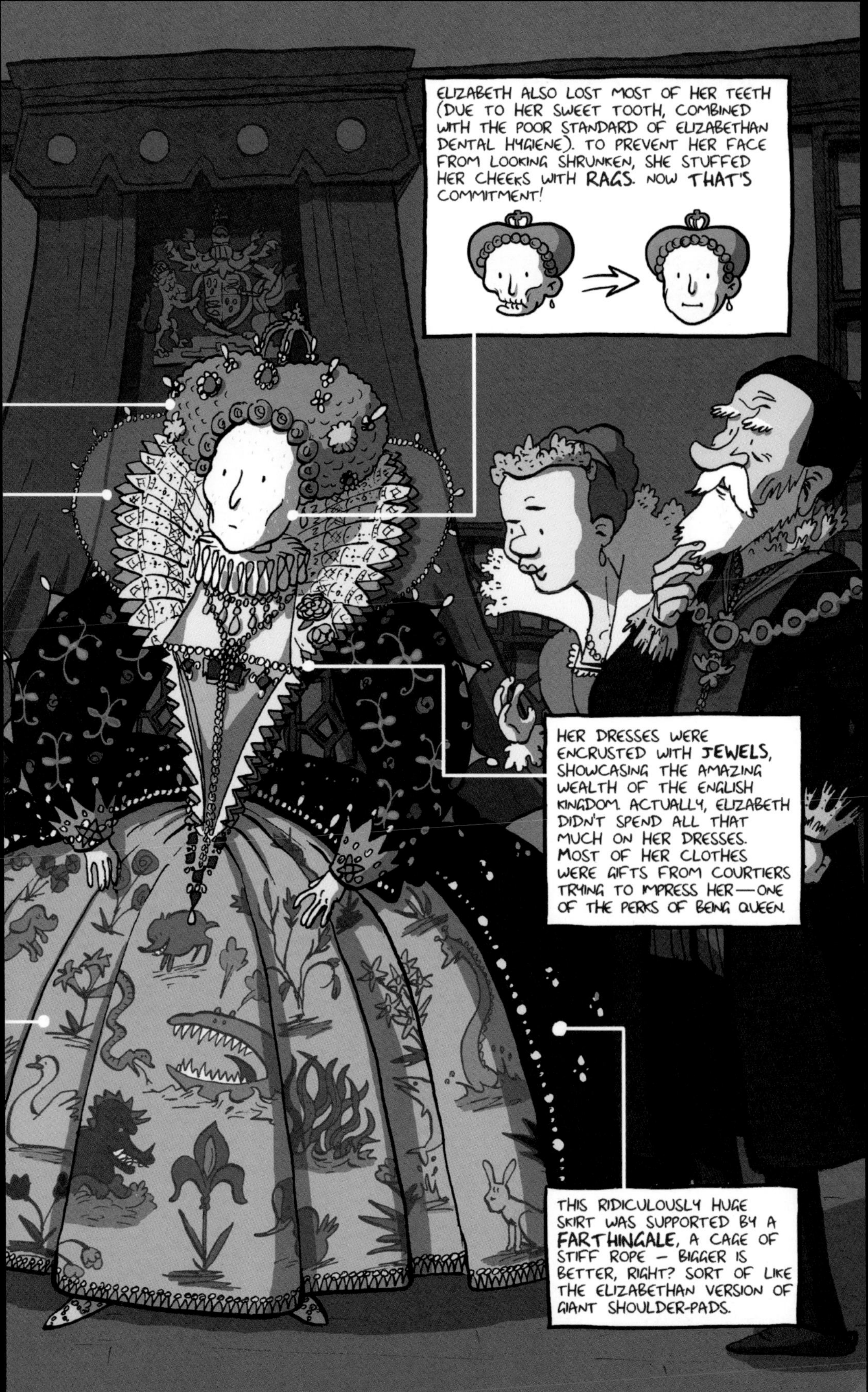
ELIZABETH ALSO LOST MOST OF HER TEETH (DUE TO HER SWEET TOOTH, COMBINED WITH THE POOR STANDARD OF ELIZABETHAN DENTAL HYGIENE). TO PREVENT HER FACE FROM LOOKING SHRUNKEN, SHE STUFFED HER CHEEKS WITH RAGS. NOW THAT'S COMMITMENT!
HER DRESSES WERE ENCRUSTED WITH JEWELS, SHOWCASING THE AMAZING WEALTH OF THE ENGLISH KINGDOM. ACTUALLY, ELIZABETH DIDN'T SPEND ALL THAT MUCH ON HER DRESSES. MOST OF HER CLOTHES WERE GIFTS FROM COURTIERS TRYING TO IMPRESS HER—ONE OF THE PERKS OF BEING QUEEN.
THIS RIDICULOUSLY HUGE SKIRT WAS SUPPORTED BY A FARTHINGALE, A CAGE OF STIFF ROPE – BIGGER IS BETTER, RIGHT? SORT OF LIKE THE ELIZABETHAN VERSION OF GIANT SHOULDER-PADS.

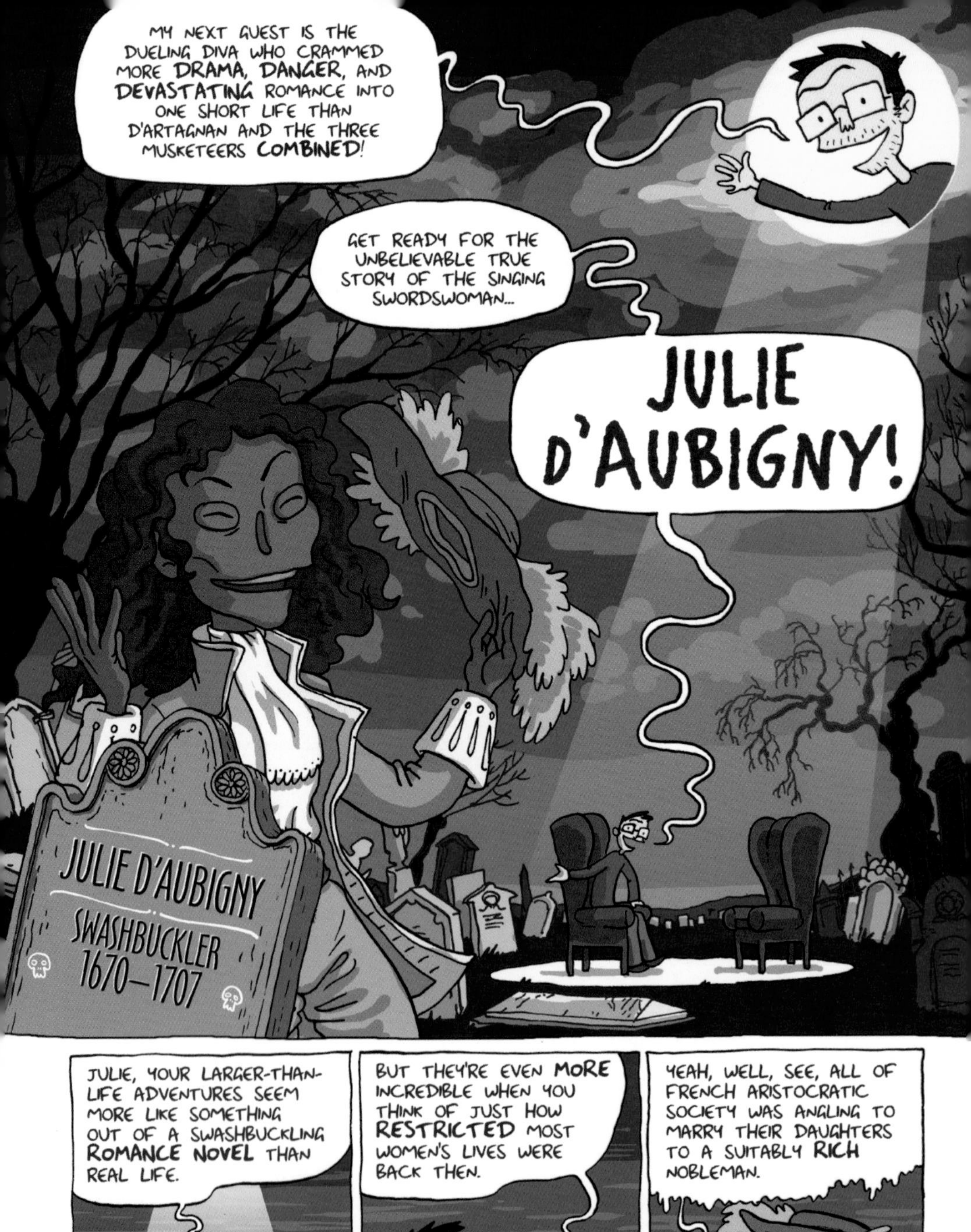
MY NEXT GUEST IS THE DUELING DIVA WHO CRAMMED MORE **DRAMA**, **DANGER**, AND **DEVASTATING** ROMANCE INTO ONE SHORT LIFE THAN D'ARTAGNAN AND THE THREE MUSKETEERS **COMBINED**!
GET READY FOR THE UNBELIEVABLE TRUE STORY OF THE SINGING SWORDSWOMAN...
JULIE D'AUBIGNY!
JULIE D'AUBIGNY
SWASHBUCKLER
1670–1707

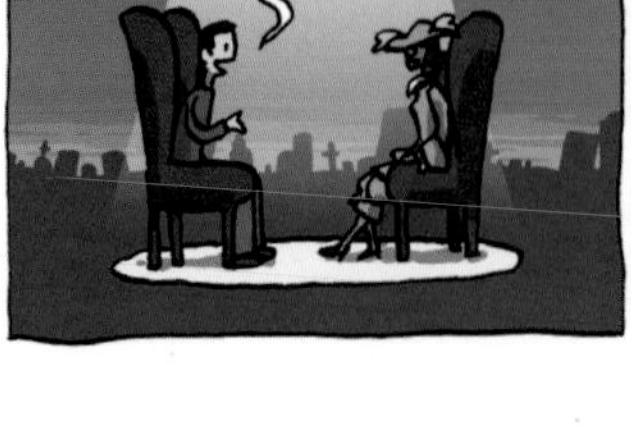
JULIE, YOUR LARGER-THAN-LIFE ADVENTURES SEEM MORE LIKE SOMETHING OUT OF A SWASHBUCKLING **ROMANCE NOVEL** THAN REAL LIFE.

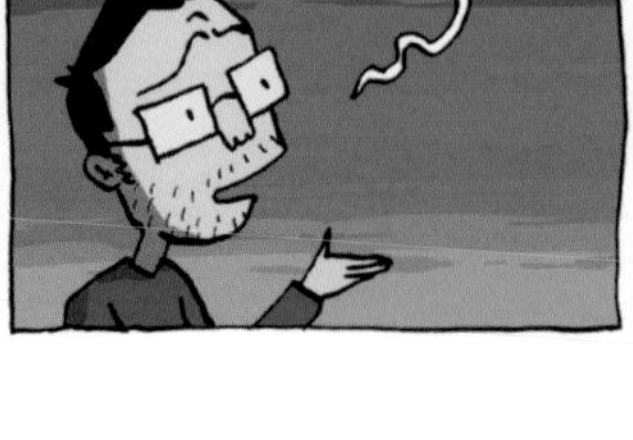
BUT THEY'RE EVEN **MORE** INCREDIBLE WHEN YOU THINK OF JUST HOW **RESTRICTED** MOST WOMEN'S LIVES WERE BACK THEN.

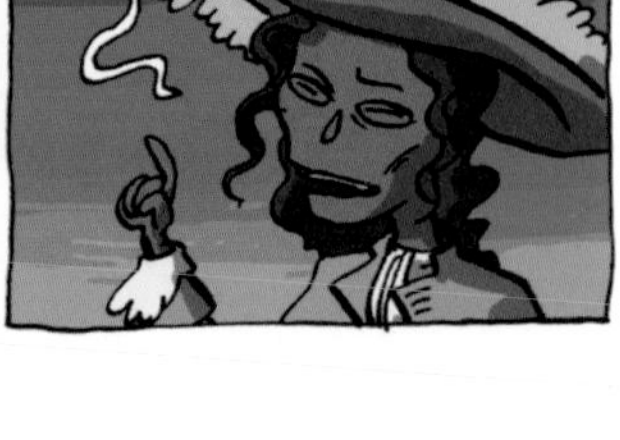
YEAH, WELL, SEE, ALL OF FRENCH ARISTOCRATIC SOCIETY WAS ANGLING TO MARRY THEIR DAUGHTERS TO A SUITABLY **RICH** NOBLEMAN.

EVERYONE WAS SO TERRIFIED OF A **SCANDAL**, GIRLS WERE KEPT UNDER CONSTANT SUPERVISION TO MAKE SURE THEY DIDN'T **MISBEHAVE**.

JUST GIRLS, MIND YOU! BOYS COULD DO WHATEVER THEY LIKED.

FLIPPIN' DOUBLE STANDARDS...

MY DAD WAS DIFFERENT, THOUGH. HE WAS THE FENCING MASTER TO THE KING'S PAGES, SO HE TRAINED ME ALONG WITH THEM.

OK, BUT EVEN **HE** CAN'T HAVE BEEN HAPPY WHEN YOU STARTED DATING HIS **BOSS**, THE POWERFUL (AND **MARRIED**) **COUNT D'ARMANAC**!

OH, PAPA **WOULD'VE** BEEN **FURIOUS** IF HE'D FOUND OUT. BUT THE COUNT HAD A CUNNING PLAN TO DIVERT SUSPICION... MY **MARRIAGE**!

WAIT. ARE YOU TELLING ME THAT YOUR **BOYFRIEND** ARRANGED FOR YOU TO MARRY SOMEONE ELSE?

YEAH. IT WAS ABSOLUTELY PERFECT. REMEMBER, EVERYONE WAS WATCHING **UNMARRIED** YOUNG WOMEN. IT WAS IMPOSSIBLE TO GO UNNOTICED!

BUT AS SOON AS I WAS MARRIED: **BOOM!** FREE PASS. ESPECIALLY SINCE LE COUNT SHIPPED MY HUBBY OFF TO COLLECT TAXES IN THE COUNTRY AS SOON AS THE WEDDING WAS OVER.

HMM. **CONVENIENT**.

FOR A WHILE. BUT I SOON GOT BORED OF THE COUNT. HE HAD THIS WEIRD OBJECTION TO ME **FIGHTING** PEOPLE...

WELL. YOUR **NEW** BOYFRIEND WAS CERTAINLY MORE EXCITING: A PROFESSIONAL SWORD FIGHTER WHO'D JUST **KILLED** A GUY.

*SIGH* SO DREAMY...

YOU WENT ON THE RUN TO MARSEILLES (SINCE DUELING WAS ILLEGAL IN PARIS. AND, Y'KNOW, KILLING PEOPLE...).

HE TRIED TO CONTINUE YOUR FENCING EDUCATION, BUT BEFORE LONG, THE PUPIL BECAME THE MASTER!

WE GAVE DUELING PERFORMANCES TO EARN A LIVING, SINGING TO ENLIVEN THE FIGHTS.

WATCH OUT! I'LL STAB YOU IN THE HEAART... ♪

DON'T MAKE ME LAUGH.

HERE: SMELL MY FAAART. ♫

BUT IT WASN'T LONG BEFORE YOU GOT BORED WITH **HIM** AND WERE IN LOVE AGAIN—THIS TIME IT WAS WITH A YOUNG WOMAN WHO YOU MET AT ONE OF YOUR DUELS.

BONJOUR...

NEEDLESS TO SAY, HER FAMILY WASN'T THRILLED.

OH MY GOD! THE SCANDAL!

NOW WE'LL NEVER GET HER MARRIED!

THEY TRIED TO HIDE HER AWAY IN A CONVENT, BUT NOTHING CAN STAND IN THE WAY OF **TRUE LOVE!**

SO, I DISGUISED MYSELF AS A NUN, STOLE A **DEAD BODY**, PUT IT IN HER BED AND SET FIRE TO THE ROOM.

HOLD ON, HOLD ON. YOU DID **WHAT?**

SO THEY'D THINK SHE DIED IN THE FIRE AND LEAVE US ALONE.

THIS IS THE MOST **INSANE** STORY I THINK I'VE EVER HEARD.

AW. THANK YOU...

AND IT JUST KEEPS GETTING CRAZIER... YOUR GIRLFRIEND DECIDED SHE WASN'T CUT OUT FOR LIFE AS A WANTED CRIMINAL, SO YOU WENT ON THE RUN BY YOURSELF...

YOU SOON FELL IN LOVE AGAIN, THIS TIME WITH A GUY YOU HAD STABBED IN A SWORD FIGHT...

YOU LEARNED OPERA SINGING FROM AN OLD DRUNK WHO WAS REALLY AN OPERA MASTER IN DISGUISE. I MEAN **SERIOUSLY**. I COULDN'T MAKE THIS STUFF UP...

THE KING PARDONED YOU FOR BEING JUST **TOO AWESOME** TO BE ARRESTED...

WHAT'S A CONVENT OR TWO BETWEEN FRIENDS!?

YOU JOINED THE PARIS OPERA AND IMMEDIATELY BECAME A **MASSIVE SUPERSTAR**...

YOU FELL IN LOVE (YET AGAIN) WITH ONE OF YOUR COSTARS AND TRIED TO **KILL YOURSELF** WHEN SHE DIDN'T RECIPROCATE...

YOU WENT ON THE RUN (YET **AGAIN**) AFTER **GATE-CRASHING** THE KING'S BALL, KISSING SOME GIRL ON THE DANCE FLOOR, THEN TAKING ON AND DEFEATING **THREE GUYS AT ONCE** IN AN ILLEGAL DUEL.

I'M GETTING DIZZY JUST TALKING ABOUT IT. DID YOU NEVER GET TIRED OF ALL THE SCANDAL?

BAH! LIFE'S TOO SHORT TO SPEND IT WORRYING WHAT PEOPLE THINK.

FOLLOW YOUR HEART! PURSUE YOUR HAPPINESS!

YEAH! YEAH!

AND IF ANYONE DOESN'T LIKE IT, JUST GIVE 'EM A GOOD **STABBING**!

NOOO! YOU CAN'T SAY THAT!

AND IT WAS ALL GOING SO **WELL**...

49

# A QUESTION OF HONOR

NOW, OUR SWORD-FIGHTING SUPERSTAR IS GOING TO EXPLAIN SOME OF THE FINER POINTS OF **THE ART OF THE DUEL.**

A DUEL ISN'T JUST ABOUT **STABBING**, IT HAS A COMPLEX SYSTEM OF RULES, ETIQUETTE, AND MANNERS...

THAT **ENDS** WITH STABBING.

IF SOME JERK HAS INSULTED YOUR HONOR, OR YOUR LADY'S, YOU'RE GONNA NEED TO **THROW DOWN.**

LITERALLY, THROW DOWN YOUR GLOVE IN FRONT OF HIM— IT'S AN UNAVOIDABLE CHALLENGE TO **FIGHT!** ONLY A **COWARD** CAN REFUSE.

BUT YOU CAN'T JUST GO AT IT (WELL, I DID ALL THE TIME, BUT YOU'RE NOT **SUPPOSED** TO). THE PROPER THING IS TO SET A DATE AND TIME.

WELL, I CAN DO TUESDAY EVENING...

MM I'M HAVING MY NAILS DONE. HOW ABOUT MONDAY?

OK, HERE'S A QUESTION: WHY DO YOU USE SUCH LITTLE SWORDS? WOULDN'T ONE OF THESE BE BETTER?

AHA! MAYBE IN A BIG BATTLE, BUT IN A ONE-ON-ONE DUEL, IT'S ALL ABOUT **SPEED.**

WHEN A **SPLIT SECOND** CAN BE THE DIFFERENCE BETWEEN LIFE AND DEATH YOU WANT A STRAIGHT LINE, NOT A BIG SWEEP!

ULP!

BAM! PINPOINT PRECISION! THAT'S A KILLING BLOW!

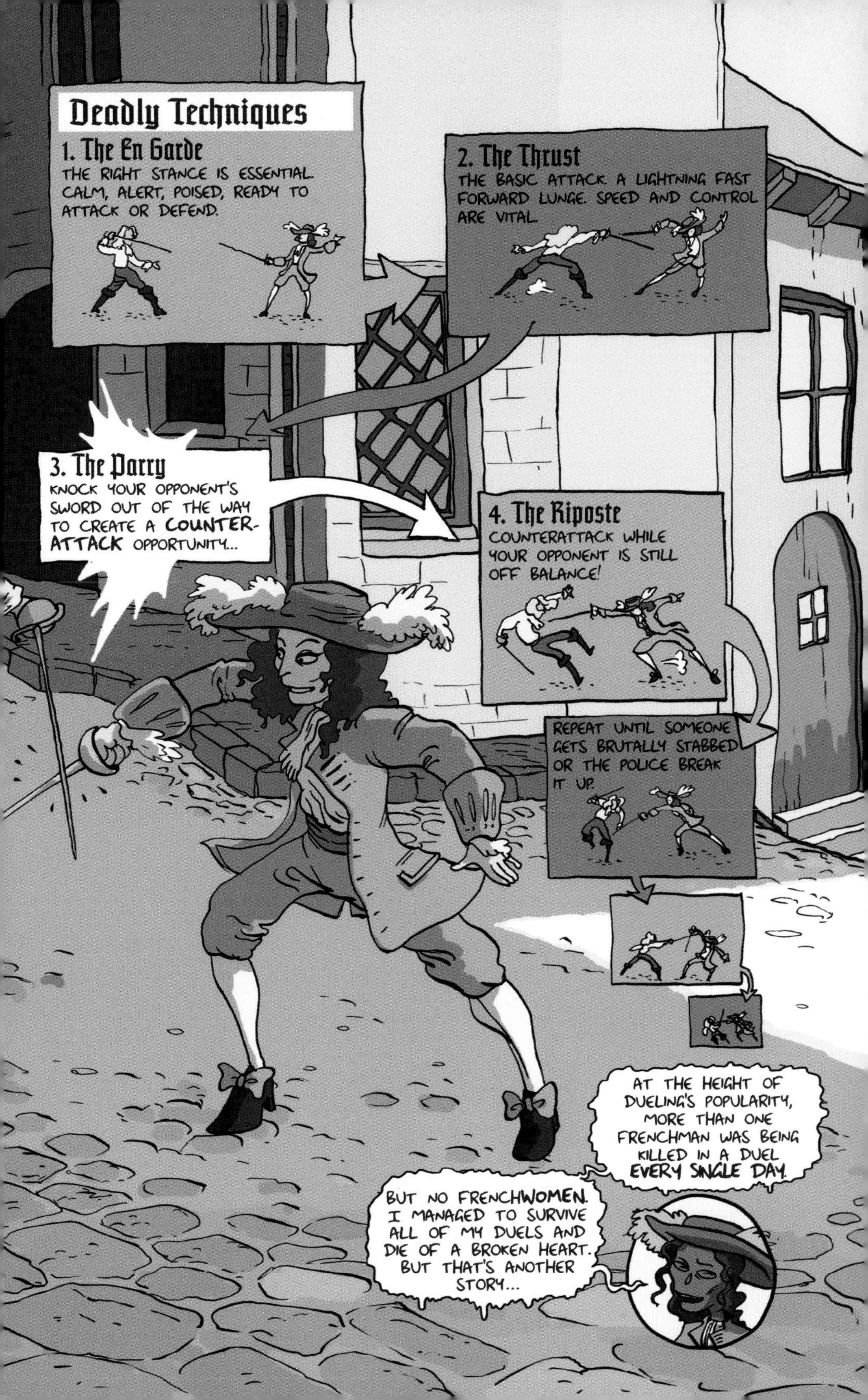
Deadly Techniques
1. The En Garde
THE RIGHT STANCE IS ESSENTIAL. CALM, ALERT, POISED, READY TO ATTACK OR DEFEND.
2. The Thrust
THE BASIC ATTACK. A LIGHTNING FAST FORWARD LUNGE. SPEED AND CONTROL ARE VITAL.
3. The Parry
KNOCK YOUR OPPONENT'S SWORD OUT OF THE WAY TO CREATE A COUNTER-ATTACK OPPORTUNITY...
4. The Riposte
COUNTERATTACK WHILE YOUR OPPONENT IS STILL OFF BALANCE!
REPEAT UNTIL SOMEONE GETS BRUTALLY STABBED OR THE POLICE BREAK IT UP.
AT THE HEIGHT OF DUELING'S POPULARITY, MORE THAN ONE FRENCHMAN WAS BEING KILLED IN A DUEL EVERY SINGLE DAY.
BUT NO FRENCHWOMEN. I MANAGED TO SURVIVE ALL OF MY DUELS AND DIE OF A BROKEN HEART. BUT THAT'S ANOTHER STORY...

I'M EXCITED TO INTRODUCE A TRUE **LEGEND**. QUITE LITERALLY: EVERYTHING WE KNOW ABOUT HER WAS PASSED DOWN IN **MYTHS AND LEGENDS.**

PLEASE WELCOME THE AWE-INSPIRING ANCESTOR OF THE **JAMAICAN NATION**, THE RIGHT EXCELLENT...

GRANNY NANNY!

GRANNY NANNY
RESISTANCE FIGHTER
1686—1755

NANNY, YOU GREW UP AS A WARRIOR PRINCESS AND MEDICINE WOMAN AMONG THE ASHANTI PEOPLE OF WEST AFRICA, WHICH I HAVE TO SAY, SOUNDS PRETTY AWESOME!

YEAH, IT **WAS**. UNTIL I GOT CAPTURED BY AN ENEMY TRIBE AND SOLD TO BRITISH **SLAVE TRADERS.**

IF THEY HAD ONLY KNOWN JUST **WHO** THEY WERE TRANSPORTING INTO THE HEART OF THE VOLATILE JAMAICAN SLAVE COMMUNITY, THEY PROBABLY WOULD'VE SENT YOU BACK!

OR TO THE BOTTOM OF THE SEA.

JAMAICA WAS A RUGGED, MOUNTAINOUS ISLAND, COVERED IN THICK JUNGLE, WHICH MEANT SMALL COMMUNITIES OF ESCAPED SLAVES, OR "MAROONS," COULD SURVIVE, HIDDEN IN THE INTERIOR.

WHY WERE THEY CALLED **MAROONS**? DID THEY ALL WEAR PURPLE?

DON'T BE SILLY.

IT COMES FROM "CIMARRON," THE SPANISH WORD FOR ESCAPED WILD HORSES. WHICH IS EXACTLY HOW THEY SAW US—AS RUNAWAY FARM ANIMALS.

BUT I **NEVER** FORGOT THAT I WAS A **FREE HUMAN BEING.** AND SO, THE FIRST CHANCE I GOT, I ESCAPED AND SET OFF TO FIND THESE MYSTERIOUS PEOPLE.

THEIR VILLAGES WERE BUILT AT THE TOP OF STEEP RAVINES, SO ANYONE APPROACHING FROM BELOW WOULD BE EASILY SPOTTED.

AHA! SPOTTED!

THE ESCAPED SLAVES WERE PASSIONATE FIGHTERS, EACH ONE READY TO **DIE** RATHER THAN RETURN TO A LIFE OF SLAVERY.

THERE WAS ONLY ONE PROBLEM... THEY WEREN'T VERY **ORGANIZED** WHEN I FOUND THEM.

SO WHEN **YOU** BROUGHT YOUR ASHANTI WARRIOR PRINCESS EXPERIENCE WITH YOU, IT WAS JUST WHAT THEY NEEDED.

I STARTED A PROPER **MILITARY TRAINING PROGRAM,** TEACHING BOYS AND GIRLS TO FIGHT.

AND I TRAINED ALL MY GUYS IN USING **PLANTS** TO CAMOUFLAGE THEMSELVES.

GOOD JOB, GUYS.

GUYS?

ARE YOU STILL THERE?

THE BRITISH ARMY HAD STARTED SENDING MILITARY EXPEDITIONS INTO THE MOUNTAINS, INTENT ON **RECAPTURING** US.

CAMOUFLAGE ALLOWED US TO GET RIGHT UP TO THE SLAVE HUNTERS AND **EAVESDROP** ON THEIR PLANS...

...SO THEN WE'LL SNEAK UP HERE...

AND THEN, USING OUR **INTIMATE** KNOWLEDGE OF THE TERRAIN, TO PICK THE PERFECT SPOT FOR AN **AMBUSH**!

THIS ONE'S MORE OF AN AM-**SHRUB**, REALLY...

BUT I ALSO REALIZED IT WASN'T ENOUGH JUST TO DEFEND OUR MOUNTAIN HIDEOUTS. WE NEEDED TO TAKE THE FIGHT TO THEM!

I ORGANIZED RAIDS ON THE PLANTATIONS TO BURN CROPS, STEAL WEAPONS AND SUPPLIES, AND TO FREE MORE SLAVES TO BOLSTER OUR RANKS.

YOU CAUSED SO MUCH DAMAGE, THAT MANY OF THE PLANTATION OWNERS SIMPLY GAVE UP AND WENT HOME.

DOES THIS MEAN WE'RE FREE?

HUH? NO. WE'RE SELLING YOU TO SOMEONE ELSE.

AFTER ALL, THE SLAVE TRADE WAS A **JOB** TO THEM—THEY ALL JUST WANTED TO MAKE THEIR FORTUNE SO THEY COULD MOVE BACK TO BRITAIN.

AH, YES. VERY HAPPY TO BE HOME.

BUT **WE** WERE FIGHTING FOR SOMETHING MORE PRECIOUS THAN MONEY OR STATUS OR EVEN LIFE ITSELF—OUR **FREEDOM**!

KNOWING YOU'D NEVER GIVE IN, THE BRITISH OFFERED YOU A **PEACE TREATY**, PROMISING TO LEAVE YOU ALONE SO LONG AS YOU STOPPED HELPING SLAVES ESCAPE.

YOUR VILLAGE (CALLED NANNY TOWN IN YOUR HONOR) WAS JUST ONE OF **SEVERAL** ESCAPED SLAVE COMMUNITIES.

LEEWARD MAROONS

WINDWARD MAROONS

Jamaica

NANNY TOWN

ALL THE OTHERS SIGNED THE TREATY, BUT YOU **REFUSED**!

AND LEAVE OUR BROTHERS AND SISTERS TO SUFFER IN CHAINS!? NOT **LIKELY**!

54

IN FAIRNESS, WE DID HAVE ONE SECRET WEAPON THE OTHER COMMUNITIES DIDN'T.

MAGIC.

MAGIC...?

I **DID** MENTION I'M ALSO A MEDICINE WOMAN...

FOR EXAMPLE, I COULD **CATCH BULLETS** OUT OF THE AIR AND THROW THEM BACK AT THE ENEMY.

GRAB!

PEOW!

PEOW!

AND I ALSO HAD MY **NANNY POT**, A CAULDRON THAT EMITTED A NOXIOUS SMOKE.

ONE BY ONE, AS THE BRITISH APPROACHED, THEY WOULD STOP TO LOOK IN, AND BE OVERWHELMED BY THE TOXIC FUMES.

OH, I SAY! WHAT'S THIS?

BUT I ALWAYS SAVED THE LAST SOLDIER, AND SENT HIM HOME TO REPORT WHAT HAD HAPPENED.

AW!

JUST A QUICK LOOK?

*AHEM* CORPSE TALK MAKES NO GUARANTEE ABOUT THE HISTORICAL ACCURACY OF LEGENDS INVOLVING **MAGIC**.

BUT IT'S PROBABLY FITTING THAT ALMOST **EVERYTHING** WE KNOW ABOUT YOU WAS PASSED DOWN BY **WORD OF MOUTH** FOR GENERATIONS.

AFTER ALL, IT'S YOUR **LEGEND** THAT INSPIRED SO **MANY** SLAVE REBELLIONS, AND IN **1833** THE BRITISH FINALLY **ABOLISHED** SLAVERY IN THEIR EMPIRE.

AND IT **ONLY** TOOK THEM A MERE **100** MORE YEARS...

TOOK THEIR TIME!

# FORTRESSES OF FREEDOM

I'VE ASKED GRANNY NANNY, TO TALK US THROUGH THE EXTRAORDINARY DEFENSES THAT ALLOWED ESCAPED SLAVE SETTLEMENTS LIKE NANNY TOWN TO HOLD OUT FOR SO LONG.

RIGHT! TO ESCAPE THE SLAVE HUNTERS, WE RETREATED DEEP INTO THE MOUNTAINS, USING THE GEOGRAPHY TO CREATE A SORT OF NATURAL CASTLE!

BY BUILDING THEIR VILLAGES AT THE TOP OF STEEP RAVINES, THEY COULD BE SURE THEY WOULD ALWAYS SEE ENEMIES COMING.

THE ONLY ROAD TO THE VILLAGE WAS ALONG THE BOTTOM OF A VERY NARROW VALLEY. SINCE INVADERS COULD ONLY PASS IN SINGLE FILE, IT MADE THEM VERY VULNERABLE TO ATTACK.

UPON SPOTTING THE ENEMY, THE ALARM WAS RAISED ON THE ABENG, A WAR BUGLE MADE FROM A GIGANTIC COW'S HORN.

IN THE COMMUNITIES, WOMEN TOOK CHARGE OF FARMING, GROWING **YAMS, PUMPKINS,** AND WHATEVER WOULD GROW IN THE HARSH, MOUNTAIN SOIL.

THE MEN HUNTED **WILD PIGS** IN THE FOREST, WHICH ALSO ALLOWED THEM TO LEARN THE COUNTRYSIDE INTIMATELY. VERY USEFUL KNOWLEDGE WHEN AMBUSHING BRITISH PATROLS!

THE FAMOUS JAMAICAN DELICACY KNOWN AS **JERK PORK** (MEAT RUBBED ALL OVER WITH SPICES AND ROASTED OVER AN OPEN FIRE) WAS INVENTED DURING THIS TIME.

**UN-**CAMOUFLAGED PEOPLE WOULD RUN AWAY, NOISILY AND CONSPICUOUSLY, DRAWING THEIR PURSUERS INTO AN **AMBUSH.**

HORNS AND DRUMS WERE ALSO USED TO SEND **SIGNALS** THE BRITISH COULDN'T UNDERSTAND. THIS ALLOWED COORDINATED COUNTERATTACKS!

THESE DEFENSIVE TACTICS PROVED **EXTRAORDINARILY** EFFECTIVE, ALLOWING YOU TO DESTROY WAVE AFTER WAVE OF SOLDIERS.

EVENTUALLY GETTING SICK OF HAVING ALL THEIR GUYS WIPED OUT, THE BRITISH CAME UP WITH A SNEAKY STRATEGY OF THEIR OWN...

IN THE MIDDLE OF THE NIGHT, THEY CARTED A BUNCH OF CANNONS TO THE TOP OF A NEARBY HILL AND OPENED FIRE ON THE TOWN.

FORTUNATELY, MANY PEOPLE MANAGED TO ESCAPE—GOING ON TO FOUND **NEW** NANNY TOWN IN A MORE REMOTE SPOT.

IT'S CALLED MOORE TOWN NOW, BUT THEY'RE STILL THERE!

AND NOW, I'M HONORED TO INTRODUCE THE LADY WHO MAPPED THE DEPTHS OF THE HEART, WITHOUT EVER LEAVING HER FAMILY HOME!

IT'S THE PEERLESS PRINCESS OF PERIOD DRAMA...

## JANE AUSTEN!

JANE AUSTEN
AUTHOR
1775—1817

JANE, YOU'RE NOW A **BILLION-DOLLAR** INDUSTRY, SPAWNING COUNTLESS BOOKS, MOVIES, AND TV SHOWS.

**REALLY?** HOW VERY GRATIFYING.

WHILE I WAS ALIVE, I WAS COMPLETELY UNKNOWN! IN FACT, I HAD TO PUBLISH MY BOOKS **ANONYMOUSLY** BECAUSE WRITING NOVELS WASN'T CONSIDERED **LADYLIKE.**

FORTUNATELY FOR ME, MY FAMILY DIDN'T CARE ABOUT STUFF LIKE THAT TOO MUCH.

WE USED TO HAVE GREAT FUN PUTTING ON PLAYS IN THE BARN—THAT'S WHERE I GOT MY START WRITING!

YOUR NOVELS FOLLOW THE TRIALS AND TRIBULATIONS OF FINDING A HUSBAND. AND YET YOU YOURSELF NEVER MARRIED. HOW COULD YOU WRITE ABOUT IT SO WELL?

JUST BECAUSE I NEVER MARRIED DOESN'T MEAN I NEVER FELL IN LOVE! I MET **TOM LEFROY** WHEN I WAS JUST **20**...

EVERY SCANDALOUS THING YOU CAN THINK OF, FROM **DANCING** TO **SITTING TOGETHER**, WE DID IT!

HEY, IT WAS A BIG DEAL FOR US BACK THEN, OK?

BEAR IN MIND, EVEN A **WHIFF** OF SCANDAL COULD SCUPPER YOUR MARRIAGE CHANCES FOR GOOD.

AND SINCE WOMEN COULDN'T **WORK**, GETTING MARRIED WAS BASICALLY THE ONLY WAY TO AVOID ENDING UP DESTITUTE.

SOUNDS CRUMMY.

YUP.

BUT YOU WERE TELLING US ABOUT TOM LEFROY. WHY DIDN'T YOU MARRY HIM?

OH, HIS FAMILY WOULDN'T ALLOW IT.

THEY DECIDED MY FAMILY WAS TOO **POOR**, SO THEY SENT HIM AWAY. I NEVER SAW HIM AGAIN.

HOW AWFUL!

I WAS **HEARTBROKEN**. HOW **DARE** THEY DECIDE ON MY FUTURE HAPPINESS LIKE THAT!

I POURED OUT MY SOUL ONTO PAPER, WRITING A NOVEL ABOUT A YOUNG LADY WHO MARRIES THE MAN SHE LOVES...

DESPITE HIS FAMILY'S OBJECTIONS!

-SNIFF!- IT BECAME YOUR MOST FAMOUS STORY, **PRIDE AND PREJUDICE!**

BUT THEN, MY HEARTACHE TURNED TO **MISERY** WHEN MY FATHER RETIRED AND MOVED OUR FAMILY TO THAT **FOUL DEN OF LIES...**

...BATH!

LOOKS LIKE A JOLLY NICE PLACE TO ME...

NO! IT'S ALL A **FAÇADE!**

THE HOUSES ARE ALL PRETTY IN THE FRONT AND UGLY BEHIND!

AND THE **PEOPLE** ARE JUST AS BAD—POLITE AND FRIENDLY TO YOUR FACE...

AND **MEAN** AND **RUDE** BEHIND YOUR BACK!

ALSO, **BATH** WAS WHERE EVERYONE WENT TO TRY AND GET **MARRIED!**

TO SEE THEM ALL ACTING **SO POLITE** WHEN REALLY THEY JUST WANTED TO FIND OUT WHO HAD THE MOST MONEY! SICKENING!

I COULDN'T GET ANY WRITING DONE THERE. I WAS MISERABLE.

 IT WAS DURING THIS TIME THAT YOU RECEIVED A PROPOSAL OF MARRIAGE YOURSELF.

 THAT'S RIGHT! WE WERE VISITING FAMILY FRIENDS WHEN THEIR YOUNGEST SON, **HARRIS BIGG-WITHER**, PROPOSED MARRIAGE TO ME.

 HE WAS RICH, AND MY FAMILY WAS QUITE POOR. IT WOULD HAVE ALLOWED ME TO SUPPORT MY PARENTS AND MY SISTER.

 BUT THERE WAS A PROBLEM...

HOW DID YOU KNOW?

WELL, YOU'RE NOT CALLED **JANE BIGG-WITHER** ARE YOU?

 WELL, YES. THERE WAS **ONE** PROBLEM. HE WAS **LOUD, STUPID,** AND **RUDE!** I COULDN'T MARRY A MAN LIKE THAT!

I CALLED IT OFF THE NEXT DAY!

SCANDALOUS!

 IT WASN'T JUST THE SCANDAL. DAD DIED SUDDENLY, NOT LONG AFTER, LEAVING MY MOM, MY SISTER, AND ME WITHOUT ANY INCOME AT ALL.

 WE WERE LUCKY: MY BROTHER FOUND US A COTTAGE ON HIS ESTATES. THOUGH WE COULD'VE JUST AS EASILY ENDED UP ON THE STREETS.

 BUT IN MY NOVELS, THE HEROINE ALWAYS FOLLOWS HER HEART! EVEN WHEN IT'S **SCARY!** EVEN WHEN IT **HURTS!**

 I FOUND LOVE IN THE STORIES AND CHARACTERS I CREATED.

 AND GAVE **MILLIONS** THE PLEASURE OF GETTING **LOST IN AN AUSTEN!**

JANE AUSTEN'S MOST FAMOUS NOVEL TAKES US BACK TO A TIME **BEFORE** WOMEN'S RIGHTS...

Jane Austen's **Pride & Prejudice** The Corpsetalk Version

WOMEN GENERALLY COULDN'T WORK OR INHERIT PROPERTY. WHICH MEANT THEIR ONLY WAY TO AVOID **POVERTY** WAS TO GET MARRIED.

BUT FOR SMART, FIESTY **ELIZABETH BENNET**, THAT'S NOT GOOD ENOUGH. SHE IS DETERMINED TO MARRY FOR LOVE, OR NOT AT ALL.

HER **DAD** HAS COMPLETELY MESSED UP HIS FINANCES. AND THE HOUSE CAN ONLY BE INHERITED BY A MALE RELATIVE. **AND** HE'S GETTING OLD. WHEN HE DIES, THEY'LL ALL BE PENNILESS AND HOMELESS!

WHICH KIND OF EXPLAINS WHY HER **MOM** IS SO UTTERLY OBSESSED WITH FINDING RICH HUSBANDS FOR HER GIRLS.

OMG! HAVE YOU HEARD!?

THE OTHER SISTERS: **JANE**, KIND AND OPTIMISTIC. **MARY**, ANTISOCIAL BOOKWORM. **LYDIA** AND **KITTY**, DITZY AND BOYS-IN-UNIFORM CRAZY.

RICH AND HANDSOME **MR. BINGLEY** JUST MOVED IN DOWN THE ROAD! AND HE'S GOING TO THE **BALL**!

GIRLS, THIS IS OUR BIG CHANCE!

AT THE BALL, MR. BINGLEY SEEMS REALLY NICE. HE AND JANE HIT IT OFF RIGHT AWAY...

BUT HIS EVEN RICHER, HANDSOMER FRIEND, **MR. DARCY**, SEEMS LIKE A PROUD-AND-PREJUDICED, STUCK-UP SNOBBY JERK.

YOU SHOULD DANCE WITH JANE'S SISTER ELIZABETH!

NOT HOT ENOUGH.

I CAN TOTALLY HEAR YOU.

JANE GOES TO VISIT MR. BINGLEY'S MANSION AND GETS CONVENIENTLY ILL, SO SHE HAS TO STAY UNTIL SHE GETS BETTER.

IT'S STILL RAINING. YOU CAN'T GO OUT IN THAT...

COUGH COUGH

SO ELIZABETH ALSO GOES TO MR. BINGLEY'S TO TAKE CARE OF HER AND SPENDS MOST OF HER TIME ARGUING WITH MR DARCY.

YOU'RE AN IDIOT!

AM NOT!

WHO IS SURPRISED AND CONFUSED BY STRANGE FEELINGS. IS THIS... ATTRACTION?

SHE REALLY JUST SAYS WHAT SHE THINKS! IMPRESSIVE...

JUST AS WELL SHE'S SO **POOR**, OR I MIGHT ACTUALLY FALL FOR HER!

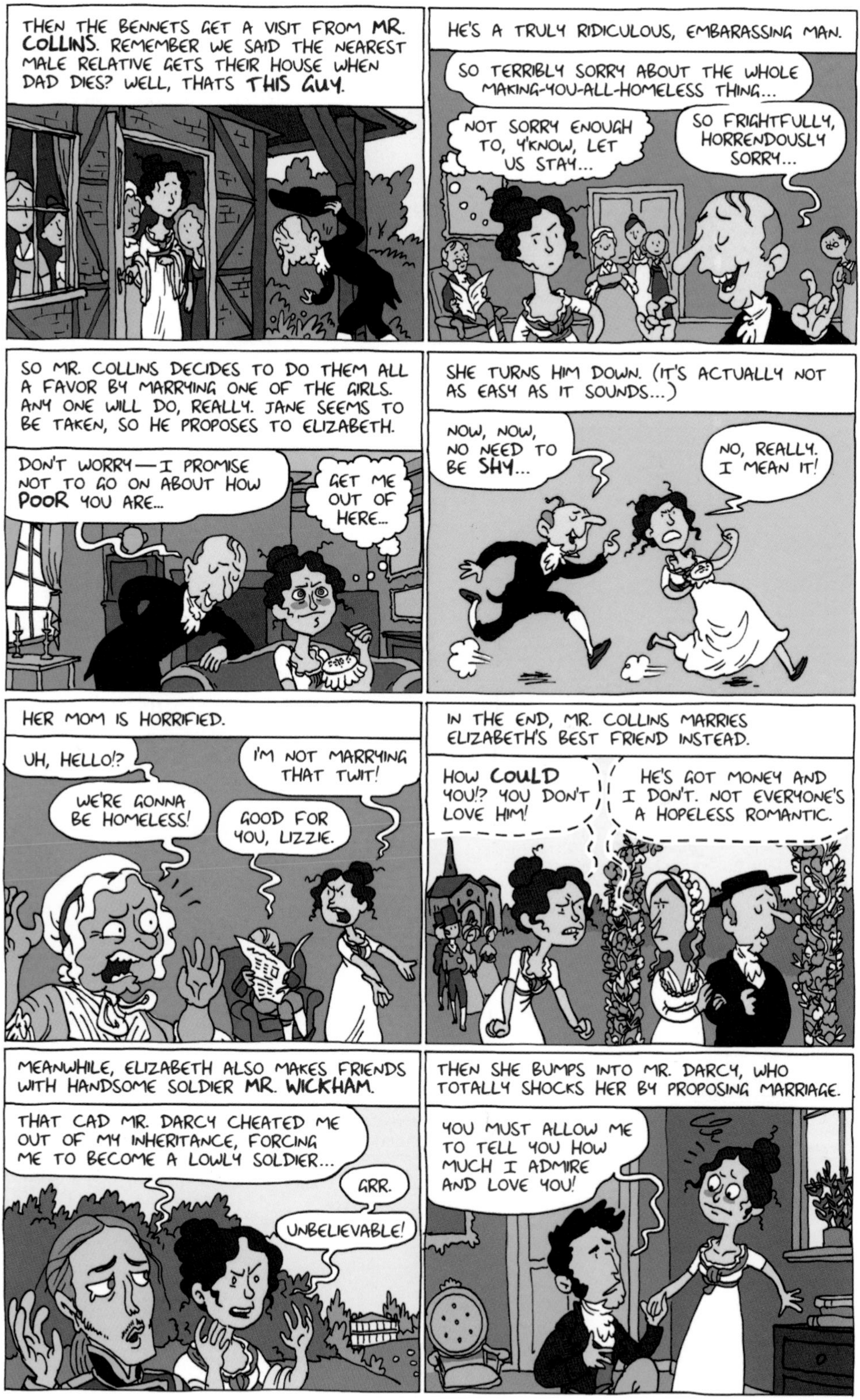
THEN THE BENNETS GET A VISIT FROM MR. COLLINS. REMEMBER WE SAID THE NEAREST MALE RELATIVE GETS THEIR HOUSE WHEN DAD DIES? WELL, THATS THIS GUY.
HE'S A TRULY RIDICULOUS, EMBARASSING MAN.
SO TERRIBLY SORRY ABOUT THE WHOLE MAKING-YOU-ALL-HOMELESS THING...
NOT SORRY ENOUGH TO, Y'KNOW, LET US STAY...
SO FRIGHTFULLY, HORRENDOUSLY SORRY...
SO MR. COLLINS DECIDES TO DO THEM ALL A FAVOR BY MARRYING ONE OF THE GIRLS. ANY ONE WILL DO, REALLY. JANE SEEMS TO BE TAKEN, SO HE PROPOSES TO ELIZABETH.
DON'T WORRY—I PROMISE NOT TO GO ON ABOUT HOW POOR YOU ARE...
GET ME OUT OF HERE...
SHE TURNS HIM DOWN. (IT'S ACTUALLY NOT AS EASY AS IT SOUNDS...)
NOW, NOW, NO NEED TO BE SHY...
NO, REALLY. I MEAN IT!
HER MOM IS HORRIFIED.
UH, HELLO!?
WE'RE GONNA BE HOMELESS!
GOOD FOR YOU, LIZZIE.
I'M NOT MARRYING THAT TWIT!
IN THE END, MR. COLLINS MARRIES ELIZABETH'S BEST FRIEND INSTEAD.
HOW COULD YOU!? YOU DON'T LOVE HIM!
HE'S GOT MONEY AND I DON'T. NOT EVERYONE'S A HOPELESS ROMANTIC.
MEANWHILE, ELIZABETH ALSO MAKES FRIENDS WITH HANDSOME SOLDIER MR. WICKHAM.
THAT CAD MR. DARCY CHEATED ME OUT OF MY INHERITANCE, FORCING ME TO BECOME A LOWLY SOLDIER...
GRR.
UNBELIEVABLE!
THEN SHE BUMPS INTO MR. DARCY, WHO TOTALLY SHOCKS HER BY PROPOSING MARRIAGE.
YOU MUST ALLOW ME TO TELL YOU HOW MUCH I ADMIRE AND LOVE YOU!

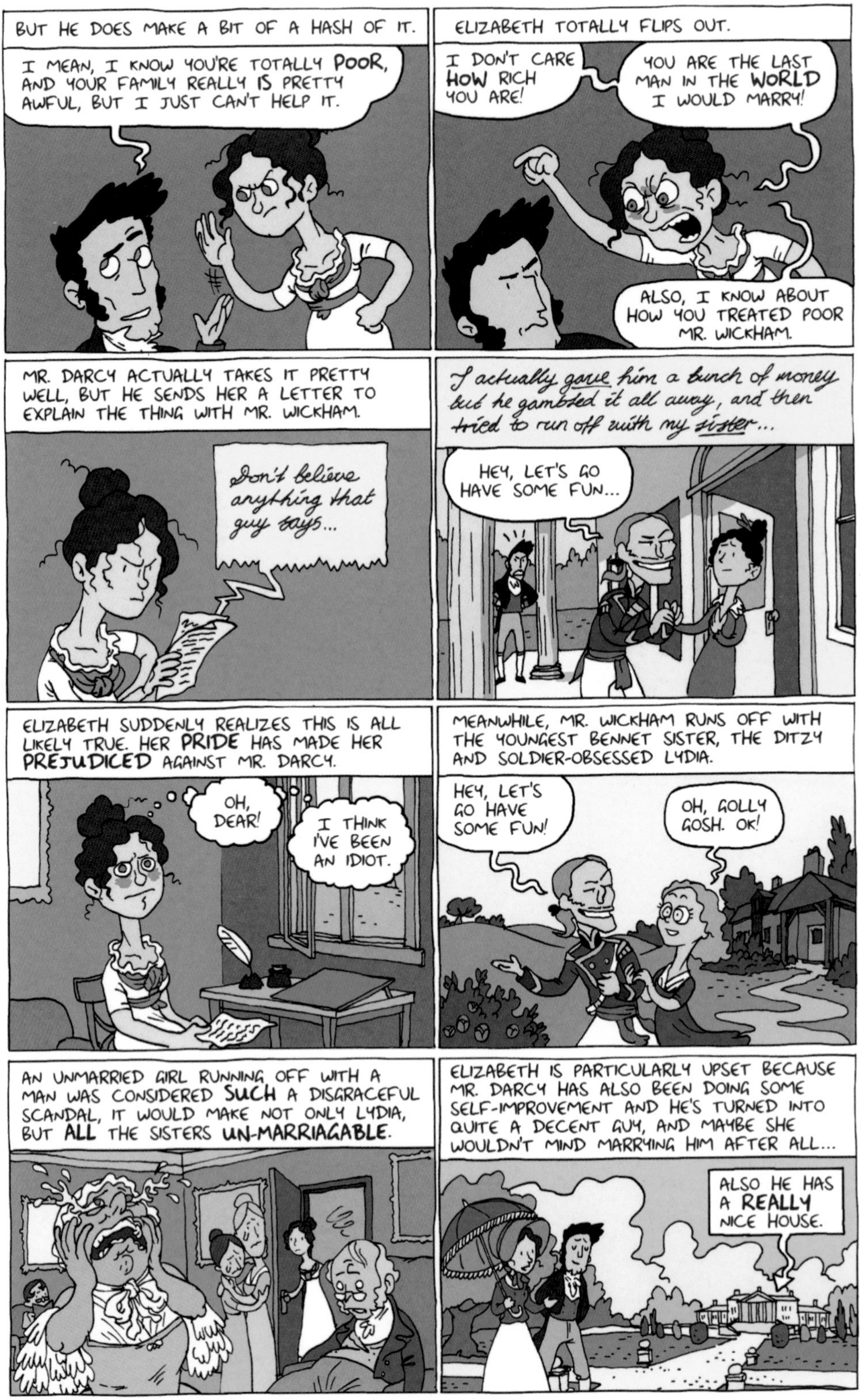
BUT HE DOES MAKE A BIT OF A HASH OF IT.
I MEAN, I KNOW YOU'RE TOTALLY POOR, AND YOUR FAMILY REALLY IS PRETTY AWFUL, BUT I JUST CAN'T HELP IT.
ELIZABETH TOTALLY FLIPS OUT.
I DON'T CARE HOW RICH YOU ARE!
YOU ARE THE LAST MAN IN THE WORLD I WOULD MARRY!
ALSO, I KNOW ABOUT HOW YOU TREATED POOR MR. WICKHAM.
MR. DARCY ACTUALLY TAKES IT PRETTY WELL, BUT HE SENDS HER A LETTER TO EXPLAIN THE THING WITH MR. WICKHAM.
Don't believe anything that guy says...
I actually gave him a bunch of money but he gambled it all away, and then tried to run off with my sister...
HEY, LET'S GO HAVE SOME FUN...
ELIZABETH SUDDENLY REALIZES THIS IS ALL LIKELY TRUE. HER PRIDE HAS MADE HER PREJUDICED AGAINST MR. DARCY.
OH, DEAR!
I THINK I'VE BEEN AN IDIOT.
MEANWHILE, MR. WICKHAM RUNS OFF WITH THE YOUNGEST BENNET SISTER, THE DITZY AND SOLDIER-OBSESSED LYDIA.
HEY, LET'S GO HAVE SOME FUN!
OH, GOLLY GOSH. OK!
AN UNMARRIED GIRL RUNNING OFF WITH A MAN WAS CONSIDERED SUCH A DISGRACEFUL SCANDAL, IT WOULD MAKE NOT ONLY LYDIA, BUT ALL THE SISTERS UN-MARRIAGABLE.
ELIZABETH IS PARTICULARLY UPSET BECAUSE MR. DARCY HAS ALSO BEEN DOING SOME SELF-IMPROVEMENT AND HE'S TURNED INTO QUITE A DECENT GUY, AND MAYBE SHE WOULDN'T MIND MARRYING HIM AFTER ALL...
ALSO HE HAS A REALLY NICE HOUSE.

THE ONLY WAY TO AVOID THE SCANDAL IS FOR MR. WICKHAM TO MARRY LYDIA. BUT THERE'S NO WAY HE'D DO THAT SINCE NO ONE KNOWS WHERE THEY ARE, AND HE'S REALLY ONLY AFTER MONEY ANYWAY.

YEAH, SHE'S TOTALLY POOR. JUST AS WELL, I'M PLANNING TO **DUMP** HER.

BUT THEN, TO EVERYONE'S SURPRISE, THEY SHOW UP AND THEY'RE ALREADY MARRIED.

ELIZABETH FINDS OUT IT WAS MR. DARCY WHO MADE IT HAPPEN.

YOU WANT THIS BOATLOAD OF CASH?

YOU MARRY THE GIRL.

AW, MAN?

NOW SHE **TOTALLY** WANTS TO MARRY HIM.

THAT WAS SO... **CONSIDERATE!**

BUT HE'S NEVER GOING TO MARRY ME **NOW**...

THEN, RANDOMLY, SHE GETS THIS WEIRD OUT-OF-THE-BLUE VISIT FROM MR DARCY'S SUPERRICH AND POWERFUL **AUNT**.

YOU ARE TO PROMISE **NEVER** TO MARRY MY NEPHEW.

BITE ME, LADY. I DO WHAT I LIKE.

HE'S GOING TO MARRY MY DAUGHTER...

THE AUNT TELLS MR. DARCY ALL ABOUT IT.

CAN YOU BELIEVE THE **IMPERTINENCE!**

HOLD ON. DOES THAT MEAN SHE'S **INTERESTED...?**

ENCOURAGED, MR. DARCY PROPOSES AGAIN. AND THIS TIME, SHE SAYS **YES.**

I THOUGHT SHE HATED HIM?

OH, DO KEEP UP.

YOU SURE ABOUT THIS? I'M A WOMAN WHO SPEAKS HER MIND, YOU KNOW.

I'M COUNTING ON IT.

JANE AND MR. BINGLEY ALSO GET MARRIED.

AND THEY ALL LIVE HAPPILY EVER AFTER!

-SNIFF- I DO LOVE A GOOD WEDDING...

MY NEXT GUEST IS THE BRILLIANT **BUCCANEER BUSINESSWOMAN** WHO MASTERMINDED THE MOST MASSIVE **PIRATE ARMADA** IN THE HISTORY OF HIGH SEAS SWASHBUCKLING!

IT'S THE SCOURGE OF THE SOUTH CHINA SEA, THE **PIRATE QUEEN**...

# CHING SHIH!

CHING SHIH
PIRATE QUEEN
1775—1844

CHING SHIH, THE EVENT THAT CHANGED YOUR LIFE FOREVER (AND LAUNCHED YOU ON YOUR UNUSUAL CAREER) WAS WHEN YOU WERE **KIDNAPPED** BY PIRATES!

YEAH. APPARENTLY **CHING I,** THE PIRATE CHIEFTAIN, HAD FALLEN IN **LOVE** WITH ME AT **FIRST SIGHT,** SO HE SENT HIS MEN TO GRAB ME.

HOW... ROMANTIC?

ISN'T IT, THOUGH?

HE BEGGED ME TO MARRY HIM. BUT I WAS NO FOOL! I REALIZED **THIS** COULD BE MY TICKET TO THE BIG TIME.

I AGREED TO MARRY HIM ON **ONE CONDITION**: AN **EVEN SPLIT**. 50% OF HIS LOOT AND EQUAL STATUS AS CO-COMMANDER OF THE FLEET.

AND THAT WAS EXACTLY THE SORT OF RUTHLESS **BUSINESS SENSE** THAT MADE YOU PROBABLY THE MOST SUCCESSFUL PIRATE LEADER OF **ALL TIME**.

YOU OVERSAW A SERIES OF CLEVER ALLIANCES AND CONQUESTS, CONVINCING ALMOST ALL THE LOCAL PIRATE CHIEFTAINS TO JOIN CHING I'S **RED FLAG FLEET**.

SOON WE CONTROLLED A MASSIVE AREA OF THE SOUTHERN CHINESE COAST, EXTORTING PROTECTION MONEY FROM THE COASTAL VILLAGES AND PASSING MERCHANT SHIPS ALIKE.

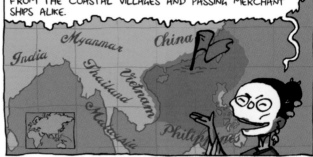

AND IF ANYONE **DIDN'T** WANT TO PAY—NO PROBLEM. WE'D JUST EXACT OUR TAXES THE **HARD** WAY.

BUT, THEN, **DISASTER** STRUCK. CHING I GOT ON THE WRONG SIDE OF AN ARGUMENT WITH A TYPHOON OFF THE VIETNAMESE COAST AND DROWNED.

ALTHOUGH HIS DEATH **DID** LEAVE ME THE UNDISPUTED MASTER OF **1,800** SHIPS AND MORE THAN **80,000** FIGHTING MEN. SO I GUESS EVERY TYPHOON HAS A SILVER LINING...

AND YOU USED YOUR NEW AUTHORITY TO CRAFT POSSIBLY THE STRICTEST AND **FAIREST** PIRATE CODE EVER.

AW, YEAH! MY FAVORITE BIT!

SO, FOR EXAMPLE: ANYONE WHO CARRIED OUT PIRATE RAIDS NOT **PERSONALLY** APPROVED BY ME—I'D CHOP OFF THEIR HEAD.

ANYONE WHO KEPT **BOOTY** FOR THEMSELVES INSTEAD OF HANDING IT INTO THE COMMUNAL TREASURY—I'D CHOP OFF THEIR HEAD.

ANYONE WHO HURT **WOMEN**—I'D CHOP OFF THEIR HEAD.

ANYONE WHO TOOK A WOMAN PRISONER—THAT'S ACTUALLY OK, SO LONG AS THEY **MARRY** HER; BUT IF THEY TREAT HER BADLY, I CHOP OFF THEIR HEAD.

ANYONE WHO RAN AWAY FROM A FIGHT...

WAIT—LET ME GUESS, IS IT HEAD-CHOPPING RELATED...?

ACTUALLY, IN **THAT** CASE, I'D CHOP OFF THEIR **EARS** AND PASS 'EM AROUND SO EVERYONE COULD LAUGH AT WHAT A **COWARD** THEY WERE.

THIS STRICT NEW PIRATE CODE TRANSFORMED THE ROWDY, UNRELIABLE PIRATES INTO A TIGHT, DISCIPLINED FIGHTING FORCE WHO FEARED **ME** FAR MORE THAN ANY ENEMY.

AND JUST AS WELL! THE CHINESE EMPEROR GOT PRETTY SICK OF HAVING A HUGE CHUNK OF HIS COUNTRY RUN BY PIRATES, SO HE SENT A MASSIVE FLEET TO TAKE YOU OUT!

THE ADMIRAL OF THE FLEET WAS CONSIDERABLY **LESS** EAGER TO TAKE ON THE MASSIVE PIRATE ARMY, SO HE BEGAN BY SAILING **FIRE SHIPS** INTO US...

WHICH WE PROMPTLY CAPTURED, PUT OUT THE FIRES, FIXED UP, AND BOOM! **40** NEW ADDITIONS TO THE FLEET!

SO, THEN THEY TRIED A FULL-ON ASSAULT. BUT WITH YOUR SUPERIOR TACTICS AND NUMBERS, YOU EASILY SURROUNDED, CAPTURED, AND **DISARMED** THEM.

ALMOST THE ENTIRE IMPERIAL NAVY AGREED TO **DEFECT** AND BECOME PIRATES INSTEAD.

WHY WOULD THEY DO THAT?

WELL, THE ALTERNATIVE WAS BEING NAILED TO THE DECK AND CLUBBED TO DEATH. SO... YEAH.

I'D LIKE TO RECONSIDER MY DECISION.

REALIZING THAT AT THIS RATE YOU'D SOON HAVE HIS **ENTIRE NAVY** UNDER YOUR COMMAND, THE EMPEROR TRIED ANOTHER APPROACH: A NAVAL BLOCKADE.

INSTEAD OF FIGHTING HEAD-ON, THE IMPERIAL NAVY PREVENTED ANY FOOD FROM BEING DELIVERED TO THE PIRATE STRONGHOLDS. SOON, THE WHOLE COMMUNITY WAS ON THE VERGE OF STARVATION.

BUT EVEN THEN YOU SHOWED THE **STRENGTH OF CHARACTER** THAT SET YOU APART FROM OTHER PIRATES.

OH, YOU!

NO, SERIOUSLY. MOST PIRATES JUST KEPT **AT IT** UNTIL THEY GOT CAPTURED OR KILLED, BUT **YOU** KNEW HOW TO QUIT WHILE YOU WERE AHEAD.

YOU WALKED INTO THE LOCAL GOVERNMENT HQ, ALONE AND UNARMED, AND PROCEEDED TO NEGOTIATE AN **INCREDIBLE** DEAL.

A **FULL PARDON** FOR ALL THE PIRATES, PLUS A NEW JOB IN EITHER THE NAVY OR, IF THEY PREFERRED, AS A FARMER.

PLUS, I GOT TO KEEP MY ILL-GOTTEN LOOT. I USED IT TO OPEN A GAMBLING DEN IN THE CITY OF CANTON.

MAKING YOU ONE OF THE ONLY PIRATES TO **RETIRE**, LIVING TO A RIPE AND COMFORTABLE OLD AGE.

NOW **THAT'S** WHAT I CALL A HAPPY ENDING!

69

# PUNKS IN JUNKS

NOW THAT YOU KNOW THE PIRATE QUEEN **CHING SHIH**, RULER OF THE RED FLAG FLEET, THE MOST PRODIGIOUS PIRATE PLATOON IN THE HISTORY OF THE HIGH SEAS, IT'S TIME TO TALK **JUNK**.

NOT **THAT** KIND OF JUNK!

WE'RE TALKING ABOUT THE **CHINESE JUNK**, THE DISTINCTIVE TYPE OF SHIP USED IN THE SOUTH CHINA SEA. SEVERAL KEY INNOVATIONS MADE THESE SHIPS FAST, STURDY, AND NIMBLE— PERFECT FOR PIRACY!

## SAILS OF THE CENTURIES

THE MOST DISTINCTIVE FEATURE OF THE JUNKS IS THEIR **SAILS**. DIFFERENT FROM THE OPEN, SQUARE SAILS OF WESTERN SHIPS, THE JUNK SAIL IS ATTACHED TO BAMBOO CROSSBEAMS OR **BATTENS**.

THESE ARE NOT NAILED TO THE MAST, BUT HANG LOOSELY ON ROPES, ALLOWING THE SAIL TO TURN TO CATCH THE WIND, OR TO BE PULLED UP AND DOWN LIKE **VENETIAN BLINDS**!

FwWwrp!

THE BATTENS ALSO MAKE THE SAILS REALLY GOOD FOR **HIDING BEHIND**, MAKING IT EASY FOR PIRATES TO SNEAK UP ON THEIR PREY DISGUISED AS FISHING BOATS.

## JUNK IN THE TRUNK

ANOTHER DISTINCTIVE FEATURE OF THE JUNK IS THESE COMPARTMENTS, OR **BULKHEADS**, RUNNING ACROSS THE WIDTH OF THE HULL. THE WALLS GIVE THE HULL EXTRA STRENGTH, AND THE SEPARATE COMPARTMENTS CAN BE USED TO CARRY DIFFERENT GOODS AND SUPPLIES.

SINCE EACH BULKHEAD IS COMPLETELY **WATERTIGHT** (THEY WERE LINED WITH A RUBBERY WATERPROOF PASTE MADE OF TUNG OIL MIXED WITH GROUND LIME) THIS WAY, IF **ONE** SPRINGS A LEAK, IT WON'T SINK THE BOAT.

IN FACT, SOMETIMES THE CAPTAIN MIGHT DELIBERATELY **FLOOD** ONE OF THE BULKHEADS. SOUNDS CRAZY, BUT THE EXTRA WEIGHT GIVES THE JUNK **BALLAST**, KEEPING IT UPRIGHT IN HEAVY WINDS.

I MEANT TO DO THAT...

JUNKS COME IN ALL SHAPES AND SIZES! MOST OF **MY** FLEET WAS MADE UP OF EITHER CONVERTED FISHING BOATS, OR ARMORED WARSHIPS WE'D CAPTURED. BUT THE BIGGEST JUNK **EVER** WAS THE FLAGSHIP OF THE CHINESE ADMIRAL **ZHENG HE**. AT ABOUT THE SAME TIME AS COLUMBUS WAS SAILING TO THE NEW WORLD, ZHENG WAS MAKING HIS OWN VOYAGE OF EXPLORATION, IN A JUNK **SO HUGE**, IT MAKES COLUMBUS'S SHIP LOOK LIKE A **LIFEBOAT**!

# ALL SORTS OF JUNK

FISHING BOAT

ARMORED JUNK

ZHENG HE'S TREASURE SHIP    COLUMBUS'S SHIP

## RED FLAG DRAGON

THE RED FLAGS OF THE RED FLAG FLEET WEREN'T JUST TO LOOK COOL. RED WAS THE FAVORITE COLOR OF THE DRAGON THE SAILORS BELIEVED LIVED IN THE CLOUDS. SINCE THIS DRAGON CONTROLS STORMS AND TYPHOONS, YOU **KNOW** YOU WANT TO STAY ON HIS GOOD SIDE!

## NOT JUST FOR VAMPIRES?

CHINESE PIRATES WOULD DOUSE THEMSELVES WITH **GARLIC WATER** BEFORE A BATTLE, SINCE THEY BELIEVED IT MADE THEM IMPERVIOUS TO BULLETS.

HE MUST'VE MISSED A SPOT.

MY NEXT GUEST IS THE IMPOSSIBLY ROMANTIC FAIRY-TALE PRINCESS WHOSE OUTLANDISH ORIGINS, ASTONISHING AROUND-THE-WORLD ADVENTURES, AND DRAMATIC DEBUT INTO ENGLISH HIGH SOCIETY SEEM ALMOST **TOO AMAZING** TO BE TRUE...

IT'S THE MISTRESS OF MAKE-BELIEVE, THE LADY OF LIES, THE ONE, THE ONLY...

## PRINCESS CARABOO!

PRINCESS CARABOO

CON-ARTIST
1791—1864

PRINCESS, YOU CREATED QUITE A STIR IN THE SLEEPY GLOUCESTERSHIRE VILLAGE OF ALMONDSBURY, WHEN YOU TURNED UP THERE SPEAKING A STRANGE LANGUAGE NO ONE COULD UNDERSTAND!

THE LOCAL MAGISTRATE'S WIFE, A MRS. WORRAL, WAS FASCINATED BY THIS MYSTERIOUS AND PENNILESS STRANGER AND TOOK YOU IN.

WORD OF HER EXOTIC GUEST BEGAN TO SPREAD AND SOON YOU WERE **INUNDATED** BY "EXPERTS" AND CURIOSITY SEEKERS, ALL TRYING TO UNRAVEL THE MYSTERY OF WHO YOU WERE.

SOME THOUGHT THAT YOUR EXCITED REACTION TO **CHINESE FURNITURE** MEANT THAT IT REMINDED YOU OF HOME.

OTHERS THOUGHT THEY RECOGNIZED SOME OF YOUR EXOTIC **DANCES** (WHICH YOU PERFORMED TO ENTERTAIN YOUR HOSTS) AS CHARACTERISTICALLY **INDIAN**.

**ONE** SELF-DECLARED EXPERT DEDUCED FROM YOUR WAY OF PRAYING BEFORE MEALS THAT YOU MUST BELONG TO A GROUP OF DISPLACED ISLAMIC REFUGEES CALLED **CIRCASSIANS**.

BUT IT WASN'T UNTIL A SAILOR RECOGNIZED YOUR LANGUAGE AS **MALAY**, THAT YOUR STRANGE STORY CAME OUT...

MY NAME, SHE SAYS, IS PRINCESS CARABOO...

I WAS KIDNAPPED BY **PIRATES** FROM MY HOME, THE FARAWAY AND EXOTIC ISLAND OF **JAVASU**.

I TRIED TO FIGHT, AND STABBED TWO OF THEM WITH MY DAGGER, BEFORE THEY OVERPOWERED ME AND CARRIED ME OFF.

THEY MADE ME THEIR SLAVE, AND FOR MANY WEARY MONTHS I ENDURED A GRUELING LIFE AT SEA.

UNTIL, UNABLE TO BEAR IT ANY LONGER, AND SEEING THE COAST OF ENGLAND IN THE DISTANCE, I JUMPED OVERBOARD AND SWAM TO SHORE.

WOW. QUITE A STORY! THOSE FOLKS MUST'VE BEEN PRETTY **STOKED**, HAVING A **GENUINE** PRINCESS IN THEIR LIVING ROOM!

OH, THEY WERE OVER THE MOON! ONLY ONE PROBLEM...

I WAS **REALLY** A SERVING MAID FROM DEVON NAMED **MARY BAKER**!

OOH! SCANDALOUS! SO THE WHOLE PRINCESS THING WAS JUST A SCAM?

I DIDN'T DO IT ON PURPOSE! THE SITUATION JUST GOT OUT OF HAND...

I'D GOTTEN FED UP WITH BEING A SERVANT. UP AT DAWN, FETCHING, CARRYING, NEVER ALLOWED TO HAVE ANY FUN. I MIGHT AS **WELL** HAVE BEEN A PIRATE'S SLAVE!

I DECIDED TO GO TO AMERICA, THE LAND OF OPPORTUNITY! MAYBE **THERE** I COULD FIND A BETTER LIFE. BUT I HAD NO JOB AND NO MONEY TO PAY THE FARE...

SO I TURNED TO THE ONLY OPTION I HAD LEFT: **BEGGING.**

OK, BUT WHY THE WHOLE PRINCESS CARABOO ACT?

I'D ALWAYS LOVED ACTING, TELLING STORIES, AND PLAYING MAKE-BELIEVE. AND I USED TO MAKE UP NONSENSE LANGUAGES TO ENTERTAIN MY FRIENDS.

BOODLY-BIP BIM-SIM...

BUT THEN I DISCOVERED PEOPLE FOUND FOREIGNERS, EVEN FAKE ONES, **FASCINATING.** AND THAT MEANT MORE MONEY!

BIDLY-BIM TAM-TOM...

SO IT WAS JUST BEGGING THAT TOOK YOU TO ALMONDSBURY?

I JUST NEEDED A FEW COINS! I DIDN'T EXPECT THEM TO TAKE IT SO SERIOUSLY!

I TRIED TO GET AWAY, TO CATCH MY BOAT TO AMERICA, BUT I'D WASTED TOO MUCH TIME BEING PRINCESS CARABOO, AND IT HAD SAILED WITHOUT ME!

SO I FIGURED I'D JUST KEEP IT UP, SEE HOW FAR IT WOULD GO.

PRETTY FAR, AS IT TURNS OUT. "PRINCESS CARABOO" WAS A **SMASH HIT,** AND I STARTED GETTING INVITED TO THE POSH PARTIES OF ENGLAND'S **HIGH SOCIETY.**

IT'S JUST **BIZARRE.** DID NO ONE SUSPECT?

WELL, I WAS VERY CAREFUL NEVER TO LET ON THAT I UNDERSTOOD ENGLISH.

PEOPLE KEPT TRYING TO CATCH ME OUT...

PRINCESS, LOOK OUT THERE!

RUN! PRINCESS, THE HOUSE IS ON FIRE!

PRINCESS, DID YOU JUST FART?

BUT THEY NEVER DID. SO EVEN IF THEY COULDN'T FIGURE OUT **WHERE I** CAME FROM, THEY NEVER SUSPECTED IT MIGHT BE **ENGLAND.**

BUT MOST OF ALL, I THINK THEY JUST BELIEVED IT BECAUSE THEY **WANTED** TO. THE IDEA OF A SHIPWRECKED PRINCESS WAS JUST **TOO GOOD** TO IGNORE!

AND WHEN THE NEWSPAPERS CAUGHT WIND OF IT, I BECAME AN INTERNATIONAL **CELEBRITY.** BUT MY FAME WAS ALSO MY DOWNFALL...

I WAS **DENOUNCED** BY A FORMER LANDLADY WHO RECOGNIZED ME IN THE NEWSPAPER.

FFFSSH!

THERE WAS A TERRIBLE SCENE WITH POOR MRS. WORRAL, THE LADY WHO'D TAKEN ME IN.

IS IT TRUE...?

BUT THEN A STRANGE THING HAPPENED: ALL THE NEWSPAPERS, INSTEAD OF CASTIGATING ME AS A FRAUD, STARTED PRAISING ME FOR GETTING ONE OVER ON ALL THOSE **RICH DUMMIES!**

WHICH WASN'T MY INTENTION EITHER. BUT I GUESS THE WHOLE THING WAS **SO** EMBARRASSING THAT IN THE END EVERYONE JUST WANTED TO GET **RID** OF ME.

I FOUND MYSELF WITH A ONE-WAY TICKET OUT OF THE LIMELIGHT AND ONTO THE LAND OF MY DREAMS—**AMERICA!**

I'LL TELL YOU WHAT I CAN'T FIGURE OUT: YOUR "LANGUAGE" WAS PURE MUMBO JUMBO, RIGHT? SO WHO THE HECK WAS THE GUY WHO "TRANSLATED" YOUR STORY?

YOU KNOW WHAT...

I HAVE **NO IDEA...**

75

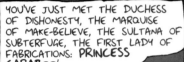

YOU'VE JUST MET THE DUCHESS OF DISHONESTY, THE MARQUISE OF MAKE-BELIEVE, THE SULTANA OF SUBTERFUGE, THE FIRST LADY OF FABRICATIONS: **PRINCESS CARABOO!**

HEH. YEAH, OK. DON'T RUB IT IN...

AND NOW SHE'S GOING TO SHARE HER SECRETS OF HOW TO MAKE UP YOUR OWN **COUNTERFEIT CHARACTER!**

RIGHT, OK. SO THIS IS...

# CARABOO'S CHARACTER CREATION COURSE!

SO, THE FIRST THING YOU NEED, IF YOU'RE GOING TO INVENT A TOTALLY FICTIONAL ALTER EGO, IS A **NAME**.

YOU NEED SOMETHING THAT SOUNDS STRANGE, BUT STILL PRONOUNCEABLE. SO BAVILAZZ OR JANDERCOO ARE GOOD, BRIAN OR XZPFLL, NOT SO MUCH.

SO NOW YOU'VE GOT A MADE-UP NAME, YOU NEED A MADE-UP **LANGUAGE**.

HERE'S HOW I MADE UP MINE!

I PRACTICED MAKING THE GESTURES AND INTONATIONS OF REAL SPEECH WHILE TALKING MADE-UP GOBBLEDEGOOK!

BLAP. BA'MBANA, CNOX AP.

BUT REMEMBER YOUR WORDS, OR PEOPLE WILL BE ON TO YOU!

SO, WHAT DID YOU CALL THIS AGAIN..?

TRY WRITING DOWN YOUR TRANSLATIONS FOR THESE COMMON WORDS:

HELLO

I COME FROM...

SORRY, I FARTED

THANK YOU

GOODBYE

MY NAME IS...

I'M HUNGRY

WHAT OTHER WORDS MIGHT BE USEFUL IN YOUR NEW LANGUAGE? YOU CAN START WRITING YOUR OWN DICTIONARY!

NEXT, YOUR MADE-UP CHARACTER NEEDS A **HOMELAND**. WHERE ARE YOU FROM? WHAT IS IT LIKE THERE? TRY COMPLETING THESE SENTENCES TO GET YOU STARTED:

THE WORDS IN GRAY ARE JUST EXAMPLES. WHAT COOL IDEAS WILL **YOU** THINK OF!?

# I COME FROM THE...

TROPICAL ISLAND/MOUNTAIN HIDEOUT/UNDERGROUND CITY/ALIEN PLANET

# OF...

WRITE THE NAME OF YOUR HOME HERE

# THE WEATHER THERE IS...

HOT AND RAINY/DRY AND WINDY/ARTIFICIAL/IT RAINS MUTANT FROGS

# WE HAVE LOTS OF...

PALM TREES/ENEMIES/PLATINUM DEPOSITS/CHEMICAL DUST

# AND...

BEAUTIFUL BIRDS/SENTRY GUNS/ROBOT SLAVES/METEOR SHOWERS

# THE PEOPLE THERE MOSTLY EAT...

PINEAPPLES/BEEF JERKY/BROILED CENTIPEDES/PICKLES

# WHAT I MISS MOST IS...

THE PERFUME OF THE TROPICAL FLOWERS/STORIES AROUND THE CAMPFIRE ON A WINTER'S NIGHT/WATCHING THE ROLLER-ARENA GAMES/MY PET SPACE-MONKEY

# I WAS...

THE PRINCESS/THE BANDIT LEADER'S GRANDCHILD/THE SACRED PRIEST-GOD/ONLY ONE OF THOUSANDS OF CLONE SLAVES

# OF...

THE NAME OF YOUR HOME

# BUT THEN, ONE DAY...

I GOT KIDNAPPED BY PIRATES/THE HIDEOUT WAS DISCOVERED BY POLICE/WE WERE INVADED BY MOLE GOBLINS/I ESCAPED MY CAPTORS AND LED A GLOBAL SLAVE REBELLION

# I TRAVELED...

IN A PIRATE SHIP/ON A WHITE HORSE/ON THE SACRED UNICYCLE OF MY PEOPLE/IN A SPACESHIP'S ESCAPE POD

# FOR...

MANY MONTHS/MANY YEARS/I DON'T EVEN KNOW HOW LONG BUT IT WAS A LONG TIME/12 LIGHT-YEARS

# UNTIL, AT LAST I...

ESCAPED/LOST MY PURSUERS/RAN OUT OF MONEY/CRASH-LANDED

# AND I ENDED UP HERE!

YOU'RE PROBABLY DRESSED IN THE NORMAL CLOTHES OF WHEREVER YOU LIVE NOW. BUT THAT'S JUST BECAUSE YOUR OWN CLOTHES WERE DAMAGED, AND YOU HAD TO BORROW SOME... RIGHT?

WHAT DOES THE TRADITIONAL COSTUME OF YOUR HOMELAND LOOK LIKE?

## ON A PIECE OF PAPER DRAW A PICTURE OF YOUR COSTUME!

ONCE YOU'VE DEVELOPED YOUR CHARACTER AND PRACTICED YOUR LANGUAGE, TRY IT OUT ON YOUR FAMILY! CAN YOU PULL THE WOOL OVER THEIR EYES? GOOD LUCK!

HABLAT! SCHICOM BEP M'NAA!*

MOM—WHO'S THIS WEIRD KID?

*GREETINGS, EARTHLINGS! FEED ME PICKLES!

AND NOW, PUT YOUR HANDS TOGETHER FOR MY NEXT AMAZING GUEST—SHE'S TOUGH AS AN ALLIGATOR AND TWICE AS ORNERY...

IT'S THE PISTOL-PACKING HARD WOMAN OF THE UNDERGROUND RAILROAD...

HARRIET TUBMAN!

HARRIET TUBMAN
ABOLITIONIST
1822—1913

HARRIET, LIKE A DIAMOND FORMING IN THE DEPTHS OF THE EARTH, YOUR UNBREAKABLE SPIRIT WAS FORGED IN THE BRUTAL SLAVE REGIME OF THE AMERICAN SOUTH.

LORD DELIVER ANYONE FROM THE LIFE OF A SLAVE. THERE'S NOTHING WORSE THAN HAVING YOUR LIFE IN SOMEONE ELSE'S HANDS.

SINCE THE MASTER OWNED YOU, HE COULD BEAT YOU WHENEVER HE LIKED, AND THERE WAS NO WAY TO COMPLAIN. WHY, ONE TIME I WAS WHIPPED FIVE TIMES BEFORE BREAKFAST.

EVEN WORSE, HE COULD SELL YOU OR HIRE YOU OUT TO ANOTHER FARM—WHICH MEANT YOU'D LIKELY NEVER SEE YOUR FAMILY AGAIN.

IT JUST SEEMS **INSANE** TO US TODAY—HOW CAN YOU CLAIM TO **OWN** A PERSON, LIKE THEY WERE A TABLE OR A CHAIR?

LUCKY YOU, YOU HAVEN'T EVER EXPERIENCED IT.

I GUESS IF EVERYONE THINKS THE SAME, IT MAKES IT EASIER TO PRETEND IT'S THE TRUTH.

WELL, NOT **EVERYONE**...

OH, SURE, IN THE NORTHERN STATES, SLAVERY WAS ILLEGAL. SOMETIMES FOLKS WOULD TRY AND GET OVER THE BORDER TO FREEDOM.

BUT THERE WERE ARMED **POSSES** HUNTING DOWN RUNAWAYS FOR THE REWARD MONEY. AND ALL THE SLAVE OWNERS WERE SURE TO TURN YOU IN, LEST IT GIVE **THEIR** SLAVES ANY IDEAS.

BUT YOU NEVER GAVE UP DREAMING OF FREEDOM.

DREAMING AND HOPING AND PRAYING FOR THE MASTER TO CHANGE HIS EVIL WAYS.

BUT HE NEVER DID. AND THEN ONE DAY, I CHANGED MY PRAYER...

LORD, IF HE ISN'T GOING TO CHANGE, LET HIM **DIE** AND LEAVE US BE.

AND WITHIN A WEEK HE WAS DEAD.

THAT'S WHEN I KNEW THE LORD WILL LOOK AFTER YOU.

BUT, WITH THE MASTER DEAD, HIS WIDOW DECIDED TO SELL OFF THE FARM, WHICH MEANT ALL THE POSSESSIONS: FURNITURE, LIVESTOCK, AND FARM MACHINERY WOULD BE SPLIT UP BETWEEN NEW OWNERS. THAT ALSO INCLUDED MY WHOLE FAMILY.

81

WELL. I FIGURED I HAD NOTHING TO LOSE NOW. AND MAYBE GOD WOULD ANSWER MY PRAYERS ONCE AGAIN.

SO THAT NIGHT, I SLIPPED AWAY ON THE RAILROAD...

CHOO! CHOO!

IT'S... UH... NOT A **REAL** RAILROAD...

THE UNDERGROUND RAILROAD WAS A LOOSE CONNECTION OF FOLKS WHO HATED SLAVERY AND WOULD HELP RUNAWAYS GET ACROSS THE BORDER TO FREEDOM.

FOLKS OFTEN WOULDN'T KNOW WHO THE NEXT LINK IN THE CHAIN WAS. IT'S SAFER THAT WAY, IN CASE YOU GET CAUGHT.

WE'D TRAVEL AT NIGHT. BUT EVEN THEN, I'D HAVE TO GO IN DISGUISE. ONCE, I WENT SEWED UP IN A FLOUR SACK.

BY DAY, I'D HIDE OUT IN THE FORESTS AND SWAMPS.

AND, THEN, ONE DAY, I REALIZED I WAS ACROSS THE BORDER! I COULDN'T BELIEVE IT! I HAD TO LOOK DOWN AT MY HANDS, TO SEE IF I WAS STILL THE SAME PERSON!

I WENT TO THE GREAT CITY OF PHILADELPHIA, WHERE I MANAGED TO LIVE DOING ODD JOBS. BUT I STILL WASN'T HAPPY.

WHY NOT?

HOW **COULD** I BE WHEN MY PEOPLE STILL WEREN'T FREE!? SO I WENT BACK INTO THE LAND OF SLAVERY TO LEAD THEM TO FREEDOM!

I FOUND I COULD MOVE AROUND UNDETECTED—WITH MY BONNET ON, PEOPLE JUST ASSUMED I WAS A SLAVE RUNNING ERRANDS.

FOLKS SANG GOSPEL SONGS WITH SECRET CODED MESSAGES SO THEY'D KNOW I WAS COMING.

♪ MOSES IS COMING... ♪ GOIN' OVER JORDAN... ♪ I'M BOUND FOR THE PROMISED LAND...

THEY CALLED ME "MOSES" BECAUSE I WAS GOING TO LEAD MY PEOPLE OUT OF SLAVERY. "JORDAN RIVER" WAS THE BOUNDARY BETWEEN SLAVERY AND FREEDOM. "THE PROMISED LAND" WAS ANYWHERE WE COULD LIVE FREE...

ANY SLAVES WHO WANTED TO ESCAPE, I'D SNEAK THEM AWAY IN THE NIGHT.

HEH, HEH. THOSE SLAVE DRIVERS MUST'VE GOTTEN A NASTY SHOCK WHEN THEY WOKE UP IN THE MORNING...

WHO'S GONNA WORK THE FARM?

WHO'S GONNA COOK MY BREAKFAST?

WHO'S GONNA PUT ON MY CLOTHES?

ALSO, THEY WERE EXTRA MAD, BECAUSE THEY WERE TRYING TO TELL THE WORLD SLAVERY WAS OK.

HEY, OUR SLAVES ARE HAPPY. YOU LIKE YOUR LIFE WITH US, RIGHT?

...

YEAH—TRY SAYING THE SLAVES ARE HAPPY WHEN THERE ARE THOUSANDS OF THEM RISKING LIFE AND LIMB TRYING TO GET AWAY.

WELL, THE LORD KEPT ON LOOKING AFTER ME: **19** MISSIONS AND MORE THAN **300** SLAVES BROUGHT TO FREEDOM. AND I NEVER LOST A PASSENGER.

ALTHOUGH, YOU LOOKED AFTER YOURSELF, TOO. YOU ALWAYS CARRIED A PISTOL IN CASE OF SLAVE HUNTERS.

WELL, THE LORD HELPS THOSE WHO HELPS THEMSELVES.

ACTUALLY IT WAS MORE FOR THE RUNAWAYS THEMSELVES. VERY OCCASIONALLY, FOLKS WOULD GET COLD FEET.

NO SERIOUSLY. THEY'RE FREEZING. I'M NOT SURE ABOUT THIS.

WHAT? AND JEOPARDIZE THE WHOLE RAILROAD!? YOU'LL **LIVE FREE OR DIE A SLAVE.**

AFTER ALL, **DEAD MEN TELL NO TALES.**

UNLESS, OF COURSE, THEY'RE ON CORPSE TALK.

83

SLAVE-SAVING HARD-WOMAN **HARRIET TUBMAN** WAS JUST ONE PART OF A LOOSE ORGANIZATION COMMITTED TO FREEING **EVERY SINGLE SLAVE** IT COULD...

# THE UNDERGROUND RAILROAD

SINCE THEY COULD BE ARRESTED OR EVEN **KILLED** FOR HELPING FLEEING SLAVES, PARTICIPANTS IN THE RAILROAD USED **SECRET CODENAMES**.

## "STATION MASTERS"

RAN **SAFE HOUSES** WHERE ESCAPING SLAVES COULD HIDE, GET SOMETHING TO EAT, AND REST UP FOR THE NEXT LEG OF THEIR JOURNEY.

**JERMAIN WESLEY LOGUEN** WAS AN ESCAPED SLAVE WHO BECAME A SCHOOLTEACHER, WRITER, ANTI-SLAVERY CAMPAIGNER, AND CHURCH MINISTER. HE HID MANY ESCAPEES IN HIS HOUSE IN SYRACUSE, NEW YORK.

## "CONDUCTORS"

WERE AGENTS LIKE ME WHO TRAVELLED WITH THE ESCAPING SLAVES, LEADING THEM FROM ONE "STATION" TO THE NEXT.

IN TOTAL, UP TO **100,000** SLAVES ESCAPED. THAT WAS STILL ONLY A TINY FRACTION OF THE **4 MILLION** SLAVES STILL HELD IN THE SOUTH, BUT AS THEY SAY: EVERY LITTLE BIT HELPS.

## "TICKET AGENTS"

WERE TRAVELERS WHO SPREAD THE WORD, LETTING SLAVES KNOW ABOUT THE UNDERGROUND RAILROAD MOVEMENT AND CONNECTING THEM WITH CONDUCTORS.

**ALEXANDER MILTON ROSS** WAS A DOCTOR AND BIRD-WATCHER. HE USED HIS HOBBY TO TRAVEL UNSUSPECTED THROUGHOUT THE SOUTH.

## "CARGO"

WAS THE SLAVES THEMSELVES. MANY WENT TO INCREDIBLE LENGTHS TO ESCAPE THE UNBEARABLE CONDITIONS OF SLAVERY.

**HENRY "BOX" BROWN** ESCAPED BY SHIPPING HIMSELF FROM RICHMOND, VIRGINIA, TO PHILADELPHIA IN A TINY PACKING CRATE!

UNORGANISED TERRITORIES

MEXICO

**"THE PROMISED LAND"**
SLAVERY WAS ILLEGAL IN THE NORTHERN UNITED STATES, BUT AFTER **1850** THEY PASSED A LAW ALLOWING SLAVE-OWNERS TO **HUNT DOWN** THEIR ESCAPED SLAVES AND TAKE THEM BACK. SO MORE AND MORE STARTED HEADING TO **BRITISH NORTH AMERICA** (OR CANADA AS IT'S NOW CALLED) WHERE SLAVERY WAS BANNED IN **1834**.

**"RAILROAD LINES"** WERE THE MAIN ROUTES THAT ESCAPING SLAVES TRAVELED ALONG.

I GENERALLY RAN MISSIONS UP FROM MARYLAND, THROUGH PHILADELPHIA, NEW YORK, ROCHESTER, AND FINALLY ACROSS THE BORDER AT NIAGARA FALLS AND INTO CANADA.

**CANADA**

HARRIET TUBMAN'S ROUTE

NIAGARA FALLS — ROCHESTER — BOSTON

CHICAGO — DETROIT — CLEVELAND — NEW YORK

**NO-SLAVERY US STATES**

BALTIMORE — PHILADELPHIA

ST. LOUIS — CINCINNATI — WASHINGTON D.C.

RICHMOND

INDIAN TERRITORY

**SLAVE-HOLDING US STATES**

GREAT DISMAL SWAMP

ATLANTIC OCEAN

CHARLESTON

SAVANNAH

NATCHEZ

OKEFENOKEE SWAMP

BAYOUS — NEW ORLEANS

NO ONE **REALLY** KNOWS WHERE THE WHOLE "RAILROAD" METAPHOR GOT STARTED. BUT IT MAKES SENSE: THERE WERE LONG ROUTES WITH LOTS OF STOPS ALONG THE WAY. AND IT WAS ALL HIDDEN FROM VIEW—HENCE THE "UNDERGROUND" PART.

EVERGLADES

CUBA

WHILE THEY STILL FACED MANY HARDSHIPS, INCLUDING INDIFFERENCE AND OUTRIGHT RACISM, FREED SLAVES WENT ON TO BUILD NEW LIVES AND BECOME A VITAL PART OF THEIR NEW COMMUNITIES.

MY NEXT GUEST WENT **HEAD OVER HEELS** (LITERALLY) IN HER EPIC CRUSADE FOR WOMEN'S RIGHTS.

IT'S THE MILITANT MARTYR OF THE SUFFRAGETTE MOVEMENT...

# EMILY WILDING DAVISON!

EMILY DAVISON
SUFFRAGETTE
1872–1913

EMILY, YOU GAVE EVERYTHING, EVEN YOUR **LIFE**, IN YOUR FIGHT TO WIN VOTES FOR WOMEN. THINGS MUST'VE BEEN PRETTY ROTTEN TO DRIVE YOU TO SUCH EXTREMES.

ROTTEN!? THEY WERE FREAKING **TERRIBLE**! WOMEN HAD NO POWER AT ALL, EVEN OVER THEIR OWN LIVES.

LIKE, FOR EXAMPLE, LEGALLY, WIVES COULDN'T OWN ANY OF THEIR OWN **STUFF**. IT ALL BELONGED TO THEIR **HUSBANDS**.

MINE MINE MINE MINE MINE MINE

IT'S JUST **BIZARRE**. HOW DID THEY GET **AWAY** WITH IT?

OH, THEY HAD LOTS OF ARGUMENTS, LIKE THAT WOMEN WERE TOO **WEAK** AND **EMOTIONAL**, FOR THE HARSH WORLD, BLAH BLAH BLAH.

BUT THE POINT IS; THIS SEXIST GARBAGE WAS THE **LAW**! AND THE ONLY PEOPLE WHO CAN CHANGE THE LAW IS THE **GOVERNMENT**.

NOW, THE GOVERNMENT HAS TO KEEP THE VOTERS HAPPY, BECAUSE IF THEY DON'T, THEY GET **VOTED OUT**.

BUT PEOPLE WHO **CAN'T VOTE** CAN'T CHANGE THE GOVERNMENT, SO THEY CAN BE SAFELY **IGNORED**.

HM. I SEE THE PROBLEM THERE. THAT'S REALLY QUITE A PICKLE...

I KNOW, RIGHT!? WELL, WE WEREN'T GOING TO BE IGNORED **ANY LONGER**!

AT FIRST, WE TRIED **REASONABLE** THINGS LIKE GIVING PETITIONS TO THE PRIME MINISTER, SHOWING JUST HOW **MANY** PEOPLE SUPPORTED OUR CAUSE.

BUT IN THE FACE OF BEING **TOTALLY** IGNORED, IT SOON ESCALATED TO DISTURBING POLITICAL MEETINGS.

OH. **VERY** MATURE...

HEY! THEY WERE MAKING DECISIONS THAT AFFECTED OUR LIVES, AND WE WEREN'T EVEN ALLOWED IN TO COMMENT ON THEM!

SO WE MADE SURE **NO ONE** COULD COMMENT...

AND FROM THERE, YOUR ACTIONS JUST GOT MORE AND MORE EXTREME. FROM SMASHING PARLIAMENT'S WINDOWS...

TO SETTING FIRE TO MAILBOXES...

HEH, HEH. THAT'S WHAT **I** CALL A **RED LETTER DAY**...

87

TO ATTACKING A DUDE YOU MISTOOK FOR TOP POLITICIAN **DAVID LLOYD GEORGE.**

OW! BUT, BUT...

DON'T **LIE** TO ME, DAVID, I KNOW IT'S YOU!

YOU WERE CARTED OFF TO PRISON FOR ASSAULTING A LOOK-A-LIKE.

NOT JUST THAT! I GOT ARRESTED FOR **ALL** OF THOSE THINGS, EVEN THE MOST **INNOCUOUS** ACTS OF PROTEST!

THEY WANTED TO TAKE AWAY EVEN THE LITTLE POWER WE HAD! WE HAD TO FIND **SOME** WAY TO FIGHT BACK.

BUT IN PRISON, WE HAD ONLY ONE TOOL LEFT— THE **HUNGER STRIKE.**

TERRIFIED OF THE BAD PUBLICITY IF SOMEONE DIED IN PRISON, THE GOVERNMENT INTRODUCED A CONTROVERSIAL POLICY OF **FORCED FEEDING.**

IT WAS THE MOST BARBARIC TORTURE IMAGINABLE! I SWORE NEVER TO GO THROUGH THAT AGAIN.

OI! OPEN THIS DOOR!

I MOST **CERTAINLY** WILL NOT.

I WAS **NOT** GOING TO LOSE THIS FIGHT.

BUT THEY EVENTUALLY KICKED DOWN THE DOOR AND FORCE-FED YOU ANYWAY.

THAT'S NOT THE POINT. IT'S NOT ABOUT WINNING OR LOSING ANY INDIVIDUAL BATTLE (I WAS FORCE-FED A HORRIFIC **49** TIMES), IT'S ABOUT CONTINUING THE FIGHT **NO MATTER WHAT.**

BUT I STARTED TO THINK, SINCE THEY'RE SO AFRAID OF SOMEONE DYING, MAYBE THAT'S WHAT IT WILL TAKE.

I WAS NOT AFRAID TO DIE. BUT IF I DIED IN PRISON, IT WOULD BE TOO EASY FOR THEM TO COVER IT UP.

I NEEDED SOMETHING **GRAND**, SOMETHING **PUBLIC**, SOMETHING NO ONE WOULD **EVER** FORGET...

SOMETHING LIKE THE **EPSOM DERBY**, THE BIGGEST HORSE-RACING EVENT OF THE YEAR.

JUST AS THE KING'S HORSE WAS PASSING ON THE FINAL LAP, I DUCKED OUT ONTO THE RACECOURSE...

I HOPE MY HEROIC ACTIONS FINALLY SHOWED THE STRENGTH, COURAGE, AND WILLPOWER WOMEN ARE CAPABLE OF!

UH... ABOUT THAT...

YOUR DEATH **ACTUALLY** GAVE AMMUNITION TO THOSE WHO WANTED TO ARGUE THAT YOU, AND BY EXTENSION **ALL** WOMEN, WERE JUST EMOTIONAL AND CRAZY!

OH, FOR GOODNESS' SAKES!

BUT YOUR COURAGEOUS ACT HAD SOWED A SEED, LITTLE BY LITTLE, YOUR CAUSE TOOK ROOT IN THE MINDS OF MEN **AND** WOMEN.

UNTIL, IN **1928**, BRITISH WOMEN **DID** WIN EQUAL VOTING RIGHTS WITH MEN.

HMPH! ABOUT DARN TIME!

# A BRIEF HISTORY OF WOMEN'S RIGHTS

RADICAL RACE-INTERRUPTING REFORMER **EMILY WILDING DAVISON** GAVE HER LIFE FOR THE CAUSE OF WOMEN'S RIGHTS. SO WE THOUGHT IT ONLY **RIGHT** TO HAVE HER **RACE** THROUGH SOME KEY MOMENTS IN THE STORY OF WOMEN'S STRUGGLE.

WELL, THE **IDEA** OF WOMEN'S RIGHTS IS REALLY QUITE A MODERN ONE.

OF COURSE, THERE WERE AMAZING WOMEN **THROUGHOUT** HISTORY (YOU'VE JUST MET SOME OF THEM!)

BUT THEY WERE GENERALLY JUST MAKING THE BEST OF THE SOCIETY THEY FOUND THEMSELVES IN...

THE IDEA THAT PEOPLE COULD **CHANGE** SOCIETY FOR THE BETTER REALLY ONLY GOT STARTED WITH THE **ENLIGHTENMENT**, THE EXPLOSION OF SCIENTIFIC AND PHILOSOPHICAL IDEAS IN THE **18**TH CENTURY.

RADICAL THINKERS DEVELOPED CRAZY NEW THEORIES LIKE "ALL MEN ARE CREATED FREE AND EQUAL IN DIGNITY AND RIGHTS".

**1791**—OLYMPE DE GOUGES, IN "DECLARATION OF THE RIGHTS OF WOMAN," POINTS OUT THAT THE **FRENCH REVOLUTION** IS IGNORING HALF OF ITS CITIZENS. SHE IS PROMPTLY **GUILLOTINED**.

WOMAN IS BORN FREE AND LIVES EQUAL TO MAN IN HER RIGHTS!

**THE PAST** ← 1770 — 1780 — 1790 — 1800 — 1810 — 1820 — 1830

**1792**—MARY WOLLSTONECRAFT, IN "VINDICATION OF THE RIGHTS OF WOMAN," ARGUES THAT WOMEN ARE AS VALUABLE AND IMPORTANT AS MEN AND HAVE THE SAME CAPACITY FOR INTELLIGENT THOUGHT.

IDEAS THAT INSPIRED THE FRENCH AND AMERICAN REVOLUTIONS AND SET THE STAGE FOR BASICALLY THE WHOLE OF **MODERN HISTORY**.

BUT THESE GUYS HAD A FUNNY TENDENCY TO FORGET ABOUT **WOMEN**.

AND BY "FUNNY" I MEAN "NOT FUNNY AT ALL."

VIRTUE CAN ONLY FLOURISH AMONG EQUALS.

**1832**—MARY SMITH PRESENTS THE FIRST **WOMEN'S SUFFRAGE\*** PETITION TO PARLIAMENT. SHE IS LAUGHED OUT OF THE HOUSE OF COMMONS.

\*"SUFFRAGE" JUST MEANS THE RIGHT TO VOTE.

THE SUFFRAGETTE MOVEMENT FOCUSED LARGELY ON GETTING WOMEN'S RIGHT TO **VOTE**. WE FIGURED WE NEEDED VOTING POWER BEFORE WE COULD CHANGE ANYTHING ELSE.

**1849**—AMELIA JENKS BLOOMER PUBLISHES **THE LILY**, THE FIRST NEWSPAPER IN THE USA SPECIFICALLY FOR WOMEN.

TRUTH IS POWERFUL AND IT PREVAILS.

**1870**—THE UK MARRIED WOMEN'S PROPERTY ACT ALLOWS MARRIED WOMEN TO OWN PROPERTY. BEFORE THIS, EVERYTHING LEGALLY BELONGED TO THEIR HUSBANDS.

SHE ALSO POPULARISES A NEW, PRACTICAL WOMEN'S OUTFIT OF BAGGY PANTALOONS, NAMED **BLOOMERS** AFTER HER.

**1851**—SOJOURNER TRUTH, IN HER FAMOUS "AIN'T I A WOMAN" SPEECH, ARGUES THAT WOMEN DESERVE EQUAL RIGHTS BECAUSE THEY WORK AS HARD AS MEN.

**1840**    **1850**    **1860**    **1870**    **1880**    **1890**    **1900**

**1869**: SUSAN B. ANTHONY AND ELIZABETH CADY STANTON FOUND THE **NATIONAL WOMAN SUFFRAGE ASSOCIATION** IN THE USA.

**1867**—THE **LONDON SOCIETY FOR WOMEN'S SUFFRAGE** IS FORMED.

FAILURE IS IMPOSSIBLE.

NOOOOOOO!

**1867**—MANCHESTER, UK, SHOP OWNER **LILLY MAXWELL** MANAGES TO CAST A VOTE AFTER HER NAME WAS ADDED TO THE ELECTION REGISTER BY ACCIDENT. HER VOTE IS LATER DECLARED ILLEGAL.

YAY!

**1893**—NEW ZEALAND BECOMES THE FIRST COUNTRY IN THE WORLD TO GIVE WOMEN THE RIGHT TO VOTE.

**1903**—EMMELINE PANKHURST AND HER DAUGHTERS FORM THE WOMEN'S SOCIAL AND POLITICAL UNION, COMMONLY KNOWN AS THE **SUFFRAGETTES**.

DEEDS NOT WORDS.

**1909**—IMPRISONED SUFFRAGETTES BEGIN **HUNGER STRIKES**. THE GOVERNMENT RESPONDS WITH A BARBARIC REGIME OF **FORCED-FEEDING**.

**1905**—SUFFRAGETTES BEGIN **MILITANT CAMPAIGNING**, INCLUDING BREAKING WINDOWS, ARSON, AND DISRUPTING POLITICAL MEETINGS.

THOSE WHO WOULD BE FREE THEMSELVES MUST STRIKE TH' BLOW

WOMEN UNITE

WOMEN OF THE WORLD

**1911**—THE **1**ST EVER **INTERNATIONAL WOMEN'S DAY** FEATURES RALLIES IN SUPPORT OF WOMEN'S RIGHT TO VOTE, HOLD PUBLIC OFFICE, WORK, AND RECEIVE AN EDUCATION. IT IS STILL CELEBRATED TODAY.

**1900**  **1910**  **1920**

WOO!

**1907**—**FINLAND** BECOMES THE FIRST COUNTRY IN THE WORLD TO ELECT FEMALE MPs.

**1913**—UTTERLY EPIC SUFFRAGETTE EMILY DAVISON DIES (TRAGICALLY AND HEROICALLY) IN A PROTEST AT THE EPSOM DERBY HORSE RACE.

WHERE ARE MY VOTES?

MR. PRESIDENT?

HUH?

**1917**—"SILENT SENTINELS" FROM THE NATIONAL WOMEN'S PARTY, BEGIN A 2-YEAR SILENT PROTEST OUTSIDE THE WHITE HOUSE.

YEE-HAH!

'BOUT TIME

**1920**—USA GIVES WOMEN THE RIGHT TO VOTE.

**1920**—CRYSTAL EASTMAN, IN "NOW WE CAN BEGIN," OUTLINES HER NEXT STEPS AFTER WINNING THE VOTE. TOP OF HER LIST: ACCESS TO FULFILLING WORK AND EDUCATION, AND ALSO **PROPER PAY** FOR WOMEN WHO CHOOSE TO BE STAY-AT-HOME MOMS.

**1929**—VIRGINIA WOOLF, IN "A ROOM OF ONE'S OWN," OUTLINES THE OBSTACLES TO WOMEN SUCCEEDING AS WRITERS AND INTELLECTUALS.

AS LONG AS SHE THINKS OF A MAN, NOBODY OBJECTS TO A WOMAN THINKING.

PUBLIC OPINION PROTECTS THE YOUNG MAN IN HIS SACRED RIGHT TO KNOW NOTHING OF HOUSEWORK.

HOORAY!

**1928**—UK GIVES WOMEN THE SAME RIGHT TO VOTE AS MEN.

**1945**—BY THE END OF WORLD WAR II, THERE ARE MORE THAN **6.5 MILLION** BRITISH WOMEN IN CIVILIAN WAR WORK. UNLIKE AFTER WWI, MANY CONTINUE TO WORK AFTER THE WAR ENDS.

**1930**          **1940**          **1960**

**1937**—BENDIX HOME APPLIANCES INTRODUCES THE FIRST AUTOMATIC WASHING MACHINE. BEFORE MODERN APPLIANCES, MARRIED WOMEN JUST DIDN'T HAVE **TIME** TAKE ON PAID WORK.

WHAT? IT'S NOT LIKE **HE'S** GOING TO DO IT...

HOME SWEET HOME

**1949**—SIMONE DE BEAUVOIR, IN "THE SECOND SEX," MAKES THE DISTINCTION BETWEEN **SEX** (BIOLOGICAL DIFFERENCES BETWEEN MEN AND WOMEN) AND **GENDER** (HOW SOCIETY EXPECTS THEM TO BEHAVE).

SHE ALSO ARGUES THAT SOCIETY'S POOR TREATMENT OF WOMEN STEMS FROM SEEING THEM AS **NOT-MEN**, RATHER THAN PEOPLE IN THEIR OWN RIGHT.

A MAN IS DEFINED AS A **HUMAN BEING** AND A WOMAN AS A **FEMALE**.

**1960**—SIRIMAVO BANDARANAIKE OF SRI LANKA BECOMES THE WORLD'S FIRST-EVER FEMALE PRIME MINISTER.

**1963**—BETTY FRIEDAN, IN "THE FEMININE MYSTIQUE," ARGUES THAT WOMEN ARE EXPECTED TO SACRIFICE THEIR CAREERS TO BE HOUSEWIVES AND MOTHERS, WHICH IS DAMAGING TO WOMEN, AND ALSO EVERYONE ELSE.

> WOMEN ARE KEPT FROM GROWING TO THEIR FULL HUMAN CAPACITIES.

**1968**—A PROTEST BY NEW YORK RADICAL WOMEN DISRUPTS THE MISS AMERICA PAGEANT. PROTESTORS ARGUE THAT GRADING WOMEN ON BEAUTY IS DEMEANING.

ALL WOMEN ARE BEAUTIFUL

MISS AMERICA CATTLE MARKET

PROTESTORS THROW BRAS, HIGH-HEELED SHOES AND OTHER SO-CALLED BEAUTY PRODUCTS IN THE TRASH. THESE **WEREN'T** BURNED, DUE TO FIRE-SAFETY REGULATIONS, BUT IT STILL SOMEHOW STARTED THE URBAN LEGEND OF "BRA-BURNING FEMINISTS."

**1960**      **1970**      **1980**      **1990**

**1975**—UK MAKES IT ILLEGAL (FOR THE FIRST TIME) FOR EMPLOYERS TO PAY WOMEN LESS FOR DOING THE SAME WORK AS MEN.

> ABOUT TIME!

**1981**—BELL HOOKS, IN "AIN'T I A WOMAN? BLACK WOMEN AND FEMINISM" ARGUES THAT FEMINISM IS MORE THAN JUST A CAMPAIGN FOR EQUALITY, BUT ALSO MEANS DESTROYING THE **SYSTEMS** (LIKE RACISM, SEXISM, POVERTY, AND SO ON) THAT ALLOW SOME GROUPS OF PEOPLE TO EXPLOIT OTHERS.

> TO BE "FEMINIST" IS TO WANT FOR ALL PEOPLE, FEMALE AND MALE, LIBERATION FROM SEXIST ROLE PATTERNS, DOMINATION, AND OPPRESSION.

**1984**—LEICHTENSTEIN BECOMES THE **FINAL** COUNTRY IN EUROPE TO ALLOW WOMEN TO VOTE.

2009—**ANITA SARKEESIAN** FOUNDS YOUTUBE CHANNEL **FEMINIST FREQUENCY** TO ANALYZE AND COMBAT SEXIST MESSAGES IN VIDEO GAMES AND TO FIGHT ONLINE HARRASSMENT.

AT LAST!

THE STRUGGLES WOMEN FACE TODAY ARE SIMULTANEOUSLY VERY, VERY OLD AND VERY NEW.

2011—**SAUDIA ARABIA** BECOMES THE **LAST** COUNTRY IN THE WORLD TO ALLOW WOMEN TO VOTE (IN LOCAL ELECTIONS).

2014—**MALALA YOUSAFZAI** (AGE **17**) BECOMES THE YOUNGEST-EVER WINNER OF THE NOBEL PEACE PRIZE. SHOT IN THE HEAD FOR BLOGGING AGAINST TALIBAN EXTREMISTS IN PAKISTAN, SHE SURVIVED AND BECAME A PASSIONATE CAMPAIGNER FOR GIRLS' RIGHTS TO EDUCATION.

WE REALIZE THE IMPORTANCE OF OUR VOICES ONLY WHEN WE ARE SILENCED.

1994—UK GUARANTEES WOMEN THE RIGHT TO **PAID MATERNITY LEAVE** FOR THE FIRST TIME.

**2000**

**2010**

THE FUTURE

WOW. WHEN I LOOK BACK AT THE CHANGES SINCE I WAS ALIVE, LIKE THAT WOMEN CAN VOTE, WORK, GET AN EDUCATION...

BUT THEN, SOME THINGS **HAVEN'T** CHANGED VERY MUCH.

FOR EXAMPLE, A GLOBAL **2015 UNITED NATIONS** REPORT FOUND THAT WOMEN EARN...

SO THERE'S CLEARLY STILL A LOT TO DO.

BUT HEY, I'VE **DONE** MY BIT! NOW IT'S UP TO YOU GUYS.

LET ME SEE HERE...

IT'S REALLY QUITE INCREDIBLE!

**24%** LESS THAN MEN, BUT WORK **15%** LONGER HOURS, AND DO **75%** MORE HOUSEWORK.

SERIOUSLY? THAT'S PREPOSTEROUS!

...WOULDN'T RECOMMEND JUMPING IN FRONT OF A HORSE THOUGH...

NOW LET'S MEET THE ONE-WOMAN **SCANDAL FACTORY** WHO WENT UNDERCOVER TO **UNCOVER UNFAIRNESS, SHATTER STEREOTYPES,** AND **BASH BIGOTRY.**

IT'S THE PIONEERING **INVESTIGATIVE** REPORTER...

# NELLIE BLY!

NELLIE BLY
JOURNALIST
1864–1922

NELLIE, YOUR GROUNDBREAKING JOURNALISM MADE YOU A HOUSEHOLD NAME IN AN ERA WHEN WOMEN WERE EXPECTED TO STAY **IN** THE HOUSEHOLD.

YEAH. BACK THEN THERE WERE ALL THESE **WEIRD** IDEAS ABOUT WHAT WOMEN COULD OR COULDN'T DO. LIKE, WE WERE SUPPOSEDLY TOO **DELICATE** TO GO OUT AND WORK.

BUT WHAT ABOUT THOSE WOMEN WHO **HAVE** TO GO OUT AND WORK!? HUH? NOT EVERYONE **HAS,** OR **WANTS,** A MAN TO LOOK AFTER THEM!

MY DAD DIED WHEN I WAS VERY YOUNG, LEAVING MY FAMILY PENNILESS. I HAD NO CHOICE BUT TO FIND A JOB!

I WAS SMART, ABLE, AND EAGER TO LEARN, BUT NO ONE WOULD GIVE ME A CHANCE!

AND THEN, ONE DAY, I READ SOME SELF-SATISFIED **TWIT** MOUTHING OFF IN THE PAPER ABOUT HOW ALL THIS IS TOTALLY FINE, 'CUZ WOMEN ARE ONLY FIT FOR CLEANING HOUSE AND RAISING BABIES.

WELL, THAT MADE ME **SO MAD,** I SAT DOWN AND SCRIBBLED OFF A FURIOUS RESPONSE.

*Dear Sir, you are a miserable fat old...*

IMAGINE MY SURPRISE WHEN, RATHER THAN AN INSULTING REPLY, I GOT INVITED TO WRITE FOR THE PAPER!

HEY, KID. I LIKE YER MOXIE, SEE?

YOU EMBARKED ON A NEW CAREER AS AN INVESTIGATIVE REPORTER, EXPOSING THE TERRIBLE INJUSTICES FACING WORKING WOMEN!

YEAH, EXCEPT THEY PRETTY QUICKLY STARTED TRYING TO MOVE ME ONTO MORE "LADYLIKE" TOPICS. LIKE CHARITY LUNCHEONS. OR FLOWER ARRANGING.

TWO WORDS: **YEAH, RIGHT!** I DITCHED THEM AND HIGHTAILED IT TO THE **HOME** OF AGGRESSIVE, CUTTHROAT, MUCKRAKING **YELLOW JOURNALISM,** NEW YORK!

I FAST-TALKED MY WAY INTO THE OFFICES OF THE **NEW YORK WORLD,** THE DIRTIEST, MUCKRAKING-EST PAPER OF ALL.

HOW'D YOU MANAGE **THAT?**

SIMPLE: I TOLD THEM I WAS INTERVIEWING **NEWSPAPER EDITORS** FOR AN ARTICLE ABOUT HOW TO BECOME A REPORTER!

WELL, YOUNG LADY, IN **MY** OPINION...

**THEY** MUST'VE LIKED YOUR MOXIE, TOO, 'CUZ IT WAS THERE THAT YOU LANDED THE JOB THAT MADE YOU A SUPERSTAR...

GOING **DEEP UNDERCOVER** TO EXPOSE THE CONDITIONS INSIDE THE NOTORIOUS BLACKWELL'S ISLAND **INSANE ASYLUM.**

THIS WAS SUPPOSEDLY A SORT OF PRISON-HOSPITAL WHERE ANYONE WHOSE BEHAVIOR WAS CONSIDERED "ABNORMAL" WAS SENT FOR TREATMENT. BUT WHAT **REALLY** WENT ON THERE? NOBODY KNEW...

RIGHT, AND IF THEY KNEW I WAS A REPORTER, I'D GET THE "OFFICIAL" TOUR. THERE WAS ONLY ONE WAY TO GET THE **REAL** STORY...

I FAKED BEING CRAZY SO THEY'D ADMIT ME AS A **PATIENT!**

NAME?

DON'T REMEMBER.

AGE?

STARING EYES.

DON'T REMEMBER.

YEP. NUTTY AS A FRUITCAKE.

I SOON DISCOVERED THAT, FAR FROM BEING A HOSPITAL FOR **TREATING** THE MENTALLY ILL, THIS PLACE WAS MORE LIKE A **TORTURE CHAMBER.**

PATIENTS WERE ROUTINELY BEATEN AND FORCED INTO FREEZING **ICE BATHS.**

THE MORE VIOLENT WERE TIED UP, WHILE THE LESS AGGRESSIVE PATIENTS (LIKE ME) WERE FORCED TO SIT STOCK-STILL, WITHOUT MAKING A SOUND, FOR HOURS ON END.

SOUNDS LIKE IT WOULD **DRIVE** YOU CRAZY, EVEN IF YOU WEREN'T ALREADY.

WELL, THAT'S THE **REALLY** SCARY THING—LOTS OF THE WOMEN IN THERE WERE AS SANE AS I WAS. BUT ONCE YOU WERE IN, THERE WAS NO WAY OUT!

FROM THE MOMENT I ARRIVED, I COMPLETELY DITCHED THE "MADWOMAN" ACT AND BEGAN ACTING SANE AGAIN.

OK, LOOK—HERE'S THE THING... SEE, I'M ACTUALLY A REPORTER...

BUT WHATEVER I SAID JUST CONFIRMED TO THEM THAT I WAS CRAZY!

HAR, HAR! A **LADY** REPORTER!

GOOD ONE!

AFTER **10** TERRIFYING DAYS, THE NEWSPAPER SENT SOMEONE TO SPRING YOU.

UH-OH.

CERTIFICATE OF NOT-CRAZINESS

MY ARTICLE, CATALOGING THE ATROCITIES I SAW, SPARKED AN **OUTRAGE**, LEADING TO A MASSIVE OVERHAUL OF THE ENTIRE MENTAL HEALTH SYSTEM.

AND CATAPULTED YOU TO **SUPERSTARDOM!** THE PUBLIC COULDN'T GET ENOUGH OF YOUR AUDACIOUS BRAND OF **STUNT JOURNALISM**.

AND YOU **USED** YOUR FAME TO HIGHLIGHT THE STORIES OF WOMEN WHO SOCIETY USUALLY PREFERRED TO IGNORE...

SLEEPING ON THE STREETS TO UNDERSTAND THE LIVES OF THE HOMELESS BETTER...

POSING AS AN UNWED MOTHER TO EXPOSE THE BLACK MARKET IN UNWANTED BABIES...

SO...

BUYING OR SELLING?

AS WELL AS MORE **SENSATIONALIST** STUNTS, LIKE TRAVELING AROUND THE WORLD IN FEWER THAN **80** DAYS, JUST TO PROVE IT COULD BE DONE!

BUT IN EVERYTHING, I SET OUT TO SHOW WHAT **ANY** GIRL WITH A BIT OF MOXIE COULD ACHIEVE, IF SHE WAS ONLY GIVEN THE CHANCE!

MAN, WHAT EVEN IS "MOXIE"?

Y'KNOW, MOXIE! LIKE, UH... GRIT...

NERVE...

CHUTZPAH...?

# 72 DAYS AROUND THE WORLD

NELLIE BLY BUILT HER GROUNDBREAKING CAREER REPORTING HARD-HITTING NEWS STORIES.

HEY, DON'T FORGET THE SHAMELESS SELF-PROMOTION! AS A **STUNT CELEBRITY** I HAD TO KEEP PERFORMING BIGGER AND BETTER STUNTS. LIKE MY RECORD-BREAKING...

AT THE TIME, EVERYONE WAS RAVING ABOUT **JULES VERNE'S** SMASH HIT NOVEL **AROUND THE WORLD IN 80 DAYS.** SO I DECIDED TO SEE IF IT WAS REALLY POSSIBLE!

**1** HOBOKEN PIER — JERSEY CITY, USA

DEPARTED NOV 14 1889, 10.55 AM

**12** SAN FRANCISCO, USA

JAN 21, 8.00 AM

SO WHAT DO YOU PACK FOR A ROUND-THE-WORLD TRIP?

I KNEW I HAD TO PACK LIGHT.

PLUS, I WAS ROYALLY **SICK** OF HEARING JOKES ABOUT WOMEN PACKING "TOO MUCH STUFF."

SO I ONLY TOOK THE BARE ESSENTIALS...

ONE SPECIALLY MADE, EXTRA-TOUGH COAT

CAP

SLIPPERS

FLASK

CUP

ONE SPECIALLY MADE, EXTRA-TOUGH DRESS

SPARE CAP

NEEDLES AND THREAD

WRITING IMPLEMENTS

TOILETRIES

A FEW HANDKERCHIEFS

BATHROBE

THREE VEILS

TENNIS BLAZER

A FEW CHANGES OF UNDERWEAR

FACE CREAM

**13**

HURRAH!

I GOT HOME AT **3:51** PM, JAN **25, 1890,** AFTER A **24,899** MILE JOURNEY, ONLY **72** DAYS, **6** HOURS, **11** MINUTES, AND **14** SECONDS AFTER I LEFT!

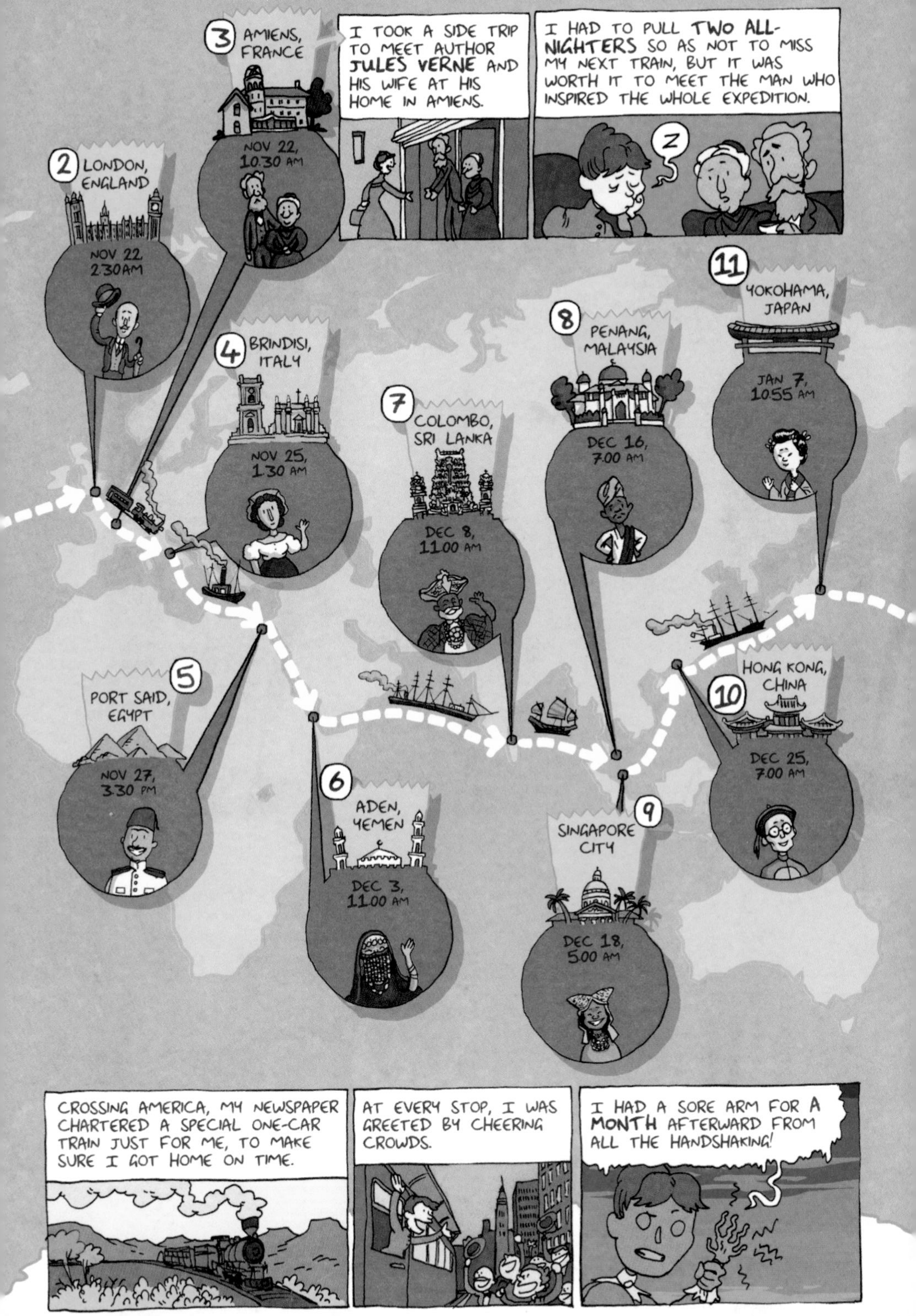
3 AMIENS, FRANCE
I TOOK A SIDE TRIP TO MEET AUTHOR JULES VERNE AND HIS WIFE AT HIS HOME IN AMIENS.
I HAD TO PULL TWO ALL-NIGHTERS SO AS NOT TO MISS MY NEXT TRAIN, BUT IT WAS WORTH IT TO MEET THE MAN WHO INSPIRED THE WHOLE EXPEDITION.
Z
NOV 22, 10.30 AM
2 LONDON, ENGLAND
NOV 22 2.30 AM
11 YOKOHAMA, JAPAN
JAN 7, 10.55 AM
8 PENANG, MALAYSIA
DEC 16, 7.00 AM
4 BRINDISI, ITALY
NOV 25, 1.30 AM
7 COLOMBO, SRI LANKA
DEC 8, 11.00 AM
5 PORT SAID, EGYPT
NOV 27, 3.30 PM
HONG KONG, CHINA
10
DEC 25, 7.00 AM
6 ADEN, YEMEN
DEC 3, 11.00 AM
9 SINGAPORE CITY
DEC 18, 5.00 AM
CROSSING AMERICA, MY NEWSPAPER CHARTERED A SPECIAL ONE-CAR TRAIN JUST FOR ME, TO MAKE SURE I GOT HOME ON TIME.
AT EVERY STOP, I WAS GREETED BY CHEERING CROWDS.
I HAD A SORE ARM FOR A MONTH AFTERWARD FROM ALL THE HANDSHAKING!

AND NOW... MY NEXT GUEST IS NO **STRANGER** TO **DANGER!** SHE CRISSCROSSED THE GLOBE ON HER HAIR-RAISING **AIRBORNE ADVENTURES.**

PLEASE WELCOME THE DARLING OF THE GOLDEN AGE OF **ENGLISH** AVIATION...

**AMY JOHNSON!**

AMY JOHNSON
AVIATOR
1903-1941

AMY, YOUR LOVE OF FLYING STARTED OUT AS AN INNOCENT HOBBY, BUT IT SOON BECAME A FULL-BLOWN **OBSESSION.**

IT GOT SO THAT I COULDN'T CONCENTRATE ON ANYTHING ELSE! WHICH DIDN'T MAKE MY EMPLOYER TOO HAPPY...

SO I DECIDED IT WAS TIME FOR A NEW JOB! **CELEBRITY AVIATRIX!**

AMELIA EARHART HAD JUST BECOME THE FIRST WOMAN TO FLY ACROSS THE ATLANTIC, AND SHE WAS IN ALL THE PAPERS. I'D HAVE TO DO ONE BETTER...

**11,000** GRUELING MILES, ALONE AND UNAIDED, IN A RICKETY SECONDHAND PLANE TO THE OTHER SIDE OF THE WORLD: **AUSTRALIA!**

LONDON
BAGHDAD | BURMA
TIMOR
AUSTRALIA

AUSTRALIA!? BUT YOU'D ONLY BEEN FLYING LESS THAN A YEAR, AND NEVER EVEN OUTSIDE ENGLAND!

PAH. DETAILS!

I PACKED ONLY THE **ESSENTIALS**: A PISTOL (IN CASE OF BANDITS), A LETTER PROMISING TO PAY RANSOM (IN CASE OF KIDNAPPERS), A CAMP STOVE, AND A SPARE PROPELLER.

I ALSO HAD A PARACHUTE. I DIDN'T THINK IT WAS NECESSARY, BUT MY **MOM** INSISTED.

MOOOOOM...

YOU HAD QUITE AN EVENTFUL JOURNEY: SANDSTORMS OUTSIDE **BAGHDAD**.

AAH! WHERE'S THE **GROUND**!?

SAND **CLOGGED UP** THE ENGINES, AND I PLUMMETED OUT OF THE SKY!

I'D NEVER BEEN SO TERRIFIED IN ALL MY LIFE!

INCREDIBLY, YOU MANAGED TO LAND IN ONE PIECE. BUT YOUR **NEXT** CRASH WASN'T SO LUCKY...

IT WAS IN **BURMA**. I CAREERED INTO A DITCH AND SMASHED A WING.

HEY! I **NEEDED** THAT!

LUCKILY, I'D CRASHED RIGHT NEXT TO THE **ENGINEERING INSTITUTE** OF BURMA! THE STUDENTS ALL PITCHED IN TO HELP CONSTRUCT A NEW WING!

OH, GOODY! EXTRA CREDIT!

THEN I HAD ANOTHER CRASH ON THE PACIFIC ISLAND OF **TIMOR**...

THE **LOCALS** WEREN'T TOO HAPPY ABOUT ME SHOWING UP UNANNOUNCED!

BUT AGAIN—STROKE OF LUCK... THEY TOOK ME TO THE LOCAL **MISSIONARY**, WHO STUFFED ME WITH WINE AND CHEESE UNTIL THE AIRSTRIP OFFICIALS SHOWED UP.

I ARRIVED IN **DARWIN, AUSTRALIA**—EXHAUSTED, SUNBURNED, BUT UNDENIABLY A **STAR**! SPONSORSHIPS, BOOK DEALS, AND PRESS TOURS BECKONED...

BUT YOUR **CRASHING** DAYS WEREN'T OVER YET...

AFTER COMING SAFELY HALFWAY AROUND THE WORLD, YOU LOST CONTROL DURING AN EASY LANDING, IN FRONT OF A HUGE CROWD, AND **TOTALED** YOUR PLANE!

HOW **EMBARRASSING**!

BUT AGAIN, YOUR LUCK HELD AND YOU ESCAPED UNHARMED.

KIND OF A RECURRING PATTERN WITH YOU— DREADFUL CRASHES FOLLOWED BY COMPLETELY **JAMMING** GOOD LUCK!

YES, I WAS VERY LUCKY FOR A WHILE. I MET MY HUSBAND, WHO WAS ALSO A FLYER, AND WE BECAME AN **AERONAUTICAL CELEBRITY COUPLE**!

BUT IT DIDN'T LAST. HE DIDN'T LIKE ME BEING MORE FAMOUS THAN HIM.

BUT THEN I READ ABOUT POOR **AMELIA EARHART** BEING LOST AT SEA...

I SWORE TO PUT FLYING BEHIND ME.

AND YOUR STORY MIGHT'VE ENDED THERE, AS YOU RETIRED TO A QUIET LIFE IN THE COUNTRY.

BUT THEN WORLD WAR II BROKE OUT! I WANTED TO DO MY BIT, SO I SIGNED UP TO TRANSPORT AIRPLANES FROM FACTORIES TO THE AIRFIELDS WHERE THEY WERE NEEDED.

IT SHOULD'VE BEEN IDEAL: A SAFE AND EASY JOB, DOING WHAT I LOVED TO HELP FIGHT HITLER.

SHOULD'VE BEEN...

BUT YOU RAN INTO TROUBLE ONE DAY, WHEN YOU LOST YOUR WAY IN THICK FOG.

AAH! WHERE AM **I**!?

UNIDENTIFIED PLANE. YOU ARE IN RESTRICTED AIRSPACE. PLEASE GIVE THE COLOR. OVER.

THE COLOR WAS A SORT OF PASSWORD. THEY CHANGED IT EVERY DAY, SO ANYONE WHO **DIDN'T** KNOW IT MUST BE AN ENEMY.

BUT I JUST COULDN'T REMEMBER IT...

RED!

NO! BLUE!

NO! WAIT A MINUTE...

I GOT SHOT DOWN BY MY **OWN PEOPLE** FOR GETTING THE ANSWER WRONG!

TEAL!

CHARTREUSE!

TAUPE!

BOOM!

BOOM!

SO YOU COULD BE THE FIRST PERSON EVER TO **FAIL** WITH FLYING COLORS!

VERY FUNNY.

FLYING ACE AMY JOHNSON MADE HER RECORD-SETING FLIGHT FROM ENGLAND TO AUSTRALIA IN HER BIPLANE, JASON, A DE HAVILLAND DH.60 GYPSY MOTH.

A **BIPLANE** HAS **TWO** SETS OF WINGS.

SO YOU HAVE A SPARE SET IN CASE ONE BREAKS!

HAR, HAR!

UH, YEAH. BASICALLY.

OK. HERE'S HOW IT WORKS...

DE HAVILLAND GYPSY MOTH

MAX SPEED: 102 MPH
CRUISE SPEED: 85 MPH
RANGE: 320 MILES

**LUGGAGE COMPARTMENT**
FOR THOSE ALL-IMPORTANT ESSENTIALS. LIKE IN-FLIGHT SNACKS.

WHERE... ARE THOSE... DARN... KETTLE CHIPS!?

**RUDDER**
FOR STEERING LEFT AND RIGHT.

**ELEVATORS**
FOR STEERING UP AND DOWN.

**AILERONS**
TO CONTROL THE ANGLE OF BANKING IN A TURN.

**SPEAKING TUBE**
BACK THEN, WE DIDN'T HAVE RADIOS OR ANYTHING LIKE THAT. A TUBE CONNECTED THE PILOT AND THE NAVIGATOR—SORT OF LIKE 2 CUPS AND A STRING!

LIFT, THE FORCE THAT KEEPS A PLANE UP, IS GENERATED BY AIR RUSHING OVER THE WINGS.

AIR

WING

AIR

BASICALLY, THE MORE WING AREA, THE MORE LIFT.

BUT IN THE EARLY DAYS OF AVIATION, THERE WAS A MAJOR PROBLEM. THEY COULDN'T MAKE WINGS LONG ENOUGH TO GIVE LIFT WITHOUT **BREAKING**!

WHICH, TRUST ME ON THIS, IS SOMETHING YOU DON'T WANT.

WHICH IS WHERE THE GREAT IDEA OF **2** WINGS CAME FROM—YOU GET DOUBLE THE AREA BUT HALF THE LENGTH!

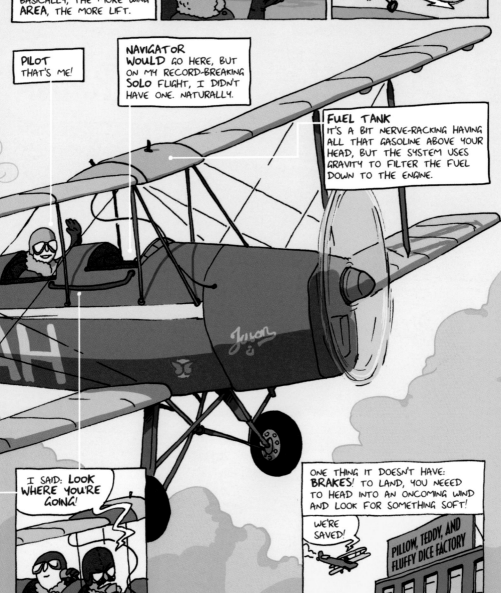

PILOT
THAT'S ME!

NAVIGATOR
**WOULD** GO HERE, BUT ON MY RECORD-BREAKING **SOLO** FLIGHT, I DIDN'T HAVE ONE. NATURALLY.

FUEL TANK
IT'S A BIT NERVE-RACKING HAVING ALL THAT GASOLINE ABOVE YOUR HEAD, BUT THE SYSTEM USES GRAVITY TO FILTER THE FUEL DOWN TO THE ENGINE.

I SAID: **LOOK WHERE YOU'RE GOING!**

ONE THING IT DOESN'T HAVE: **BRAKES!** TO LAND, YOU NEED TO HEAD INTO AN ONCOMING WIND AND LOOK FOR SOMETHING SOFT!

WE'RE SAVED!

PILLOW, TEDDY, AND FLUFFY DICE FACTORY

NEXT, I'M TALKING TO THE WORLD'S BEST-KNOWN YOUNG WRITER, AND ALSO THE YOUNGEST GUEST WE'VE EVER HAD ON THE SHOW (SINCE SHE DIED AT THE AGE OF JUST **15**).

IT'S THE GIRL WHO GAVE US A GLIMPSE INSIDE THE GENOCIDE* COMMITTED BY NAZI GERMANY...

# ANNE FRANK!

ANNE FRANK
DIARIST
1929–1945

ANNE, YOUR FAMILY WENT INTO HIDING TO ESCAPE THE **NAZIS**, RACIST THUGS WHO WERE HUNTING AND PERSECUTING JEWS ALL ACROSS EUROPE.

WHAT WAS THEIR **PROBLEM**?

SOME PEOPLE JUST NEED TO HAVE SOMEONE TO PICK ON. AND THEY DECIDED TO PICK ON JEWS LIKE US.

*GENOCIDE: THE MASS MURDER OF A PARTICULAR GROUP OF PEOPLE.

WHEN HITLER (THE CHIEF NAZI) CAME TO POWER IN GERMANY, MY DAD REALIZED THINGS WERE GOING TO GET UGLY, SO HE MOVED US ALL TO THE NETHERLANDS. I WAS ONLY **FOUR** AT THE TIME.

BUT THEN WHEN **WWII*** STARTED, THEY INVADED THE NETHERLANDS AND TOOK IT OVER!

MUST'VE BEEN TERRIFYING...

WELL, AT FIRST THEY TOLD US NOT TO WORRY—THEY JUST WANTED TO "ORGANIZE" THINGS BETTER, SO ALL THE JEWS HAD TO REGISTER AND CARRY ID CARDS.

BUT THEN THEY STARTED MAKING MORE AND MORE ANTI-JEWISH LAWS. I HAD TO LEAVE ALL MY FRIENDS BEHIND TO GO TO AN ALL-JEWISH SCHOOL.

THEN THINGS STARTED GETTING CRAZY. LIKE, THEY SAID JEWS COULDN'T DRIVE CARS, TAKE THE BUS, OR OWN BICYCLES! SO WE HAD TO **WALK** EVERYWHERE.

JEWS WERE GETTING BEATEN UP, ARRESTED, OR TAKEN AWAY, NO ONE KNEW WHERE!

THEN WE GOT A LETTER SAYING THEY WERE GOING TO TAKE MY SISTER AWAY.

NO **WAY** THAT'S HAPPENING! I'VE GOT A PLAN...

MY DAD

HE'D CONVERTED SOME UNUSED ROOMS BEHIND HIS COMPANY'S OFFICE INTO A SECRET LITTLE HOUSE!

HIDDEN DOOR

WE LEFT THAT NIGHT. WE COULDN'T BE SEEN WITH SUITCASES, IN CASE SOMEONE THOUGHT WE WERE RUNNING AWAY, SO WE HAD TO WEAR ALL OUR CLOTHES AT ONCE!

LOVELY NIGHT, OFFICER.

YOU STAYED HIDDEN IN THAT SECRET HOUSE, WITHOUT EVER COMING OUT, FOR **TWO** YEARS! YOU MUST'VE BEEN GOING CRAZY!

WE HAD TO BE SUPER-QUIET ALL THE TIME, IN CASE SOMEONE HEARD AND DISCOVERED US. IT WAS REALLY HARD FOR A CHATTERBOX LIKE ME!

\* "WWII" STANDS FOR WORLD WAR TWO.

ALSO, WE TOOK IN **FOUR** MORE PEOPLE, SO IT WAS VERY CROWDED.

MR. FRANK

MRS. FRANK

MRS. VAN PELS

MARGOT FRANK

MR. VAN PELS

ANNE

PETER VAN PELS

FRITZ PFEFFER

**VERY QUICKLY** WE ALL STARTED GETTING ON EACH OTHER'S NERVES.

MRS. VAN PELS WAS A TOTAL TROUBLEMAKER— SHE WAS ALWAYS PICKING FIGHTS. OR, EVEN WORSE, GETTING OTHER PEOPLE FIGHTING, AND THEN SITTING BACK AND ENJOYING IT!

FRITZ PFEFFER WAS A SELFISH PIG! HE WOULD LOCK HIMSELF IN THE TOILET FOR HOURS ON END, NO MATTER WHO WAS WAITING OUTSIDE!

AND DON'T EVEN GET ME **STARTED** ON MY MOTHER! WHENEVER I NEEDED SUPPORT OR A KIND WORD, SHE COULD BE GUARANTEED TO CUT ME DOWN!

GEEZ, DON'T HOLD BACK, EH, ANNE!? TELL US WHAT YOU REALLY THINK!

HEY, LOOK. I JUST WANTED TO BE HONEST! SO I'D TELL PEOPLE RIGHT TO THEIR FACES WHAT I THOUGHT.

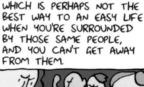

WHICH IS PERHAPS NOT THE BEST WAY TO AN EASY LIFE WHEN YOU'RE SURROUNDED BY THOSE SAME PEOPLE, AND YOU CAN'T GET AWAY FROM THEM.

SO, WITH NO OTHER OUTLETS, YOU IMMERSED YOURSELF IN YOUR WRITING.

MY GOD! IT WAS MY SALVATION!

NO MATTER HOW CRAZY THINGS GOT, I KNEW I COULD POUR OUT MY HEART IN MY WRITING AND MY DIARY WOULD ALWAYS LISTEN AND UNDERSTAND.

AT FIRST, I WAS DETERMINED **NEVER** TO LET ANYONE SEE WHAT I WAS WRITING.

JUST A **LITTLE** PEEK...?

SLAM!

JUST FINISHED WRITING SOMETHING MEAN ABOUT **HER**!

BUT ONE DAY I HEARD ON THE RADIO (WE LISTENED IN THE EVENINGS WITH THE VOLUME TURNED LOW) ABOUT A PLAN TO **COLLECT** PEOPLE'S STORIES AFTER THE WAR.

I REALIZED THAT THIS COULD BE MY CHANCE TO FULFILL MY GREAT AMBITION AND BECOME A REAL, FAMOUS AUTHOR!

SO YOU MIGHT BE PLEASED TO KNOW THAT YOUR DIARY HAS SOLD MORE THAT **30 MILLION** COPIES AND BEEN TRANSLATED INTO OVER **70** LANGUAGES!

NO WAY! THAT'S AWESOME!

BUT, ALAS, YOU DIDN'T LIVE TO SEE IT. SOMEONE (TO THIS DAY, NO ONE KNOWS WHO) FOUND OUT ABOUT YOUR HIDING PLACE AND TOLD THE GERMAN SECRET POLICE.

THEY ARRESTED EVERYONE AND SENT YOU TO THE **CONCENTRATION CAMPS**: THE **FACTORIES OF DEATH** WHERE THE NAZIS KILLED AN UNBELIEVABLE **SIX MILLION** JEWS.

THIS MONSTROUS MASS MURDER, THE **HOLOCAUST**, WAS THE LARGEST AND MOST THOROUGH ATTEMPT IN HISTORY TO COMPLETELY **ANNIHILATE** A GROUP OF PEOPLE.

MAYBE THAT'S WHY YOUR DIARY HAS SUCH AN IMPACT. YOU SEEM SO TOTALLY **UNREMARKABLE** ON THE OUTSIDE—JUST AN ORDINARY GIRL.

THANKS...

BUT IT'S THE **RADIANT INNER LIFE** REVEALED IN YOUR DIARY THAT MAKES US REALIZE THAT **EVERY ONE** OF THOSE SIX MILLION WHO DIED ALSO HAD LOVES AND HOPES AND DREAMS, JUST AS YOU DID.

IT'S JUST... SO **AWFUL**. HOW CAN WE GO ON LIVING? HOW CAN WE **EVER** HOPE FOR HAPPINESS EVER AGAIN...

DON'T GIVE UP! I ALWAYS SAID, DESPITE EVERYTHING, I TRULY BELIEVE THAT PEOPLE ARE **GOOD AT HEART**. THINK OF ALL THE BEAUTY THAT STILL REMAINS, AND TAKE COURAGE FROM THAT.

111

# THE SECRET ANNEX

NOW, HERE'S AN IN-DEPTH LOOK INSIDE ANNE FRANK'S **SECRET ANNEX**, THE HIDING PLACE BEHIND HER FATHER'S OFFICE WHERE SHE AND HER FAMILY HID FROM THE NAZIS DURING **WWII**.

THE OFFICE WAS A VERY BUSY PLACE, TEEMING WITH WORKERS, CUSTOMERS, AND BUSINESS PEOPLE, ANY **ONE** OF WHOM COULD HAVE GIVEN THE GAME AWAY. HIDING HERE WAS LIKE A DEADLY, 2-YEAR-LONG GAME OF **HIDE AND SEEK**.

## THE HELPERS

THE HIDERS WOULDN'T HAVE SURVIVED WITHOUT A COURAGEOUS GROUP OF HELPERS (ALL OF WHOM FACED ARREST OR EVEN **DEATH** IF THEY WERE CAUGHT).

**MIEP GIES.** OTTO FRANK'S COMPANY SECRETARY. SHE SECRETLY SMUGGLED IN BLACK-MARKET FOOD.

**FRONT ATTIC**

WORKERS WERE TOLD THE BACK WINDOWS WERE PAINTED OVER TO PROTECT THE STOREROOM SPICES FROM THE SUN, BUT REALLY IT WAS SO NO ONE COULD SEE INTO THE SECRET ANNEX.

**STOREROOMS**

IT WAS ALSO MIEP WHO SAVED ANNE'S PRECIOUS DIARY, HOPING ONE DAY TO RETURN IT TO HER.

**OFFICES**

THE HELPERS WHO WORKED IN THE OFFICE NEVER MENTIONED THE HIDERS, IN CASE SOMEONE OVERHEARD THEM.

**VICTOR KUGLER.** OTTO FRANK'S RIGHT-HAND MAN. FIDDLED THE ACCOUNTS SO NO ONE WOULD NOTICE ALL THE MONEY THAT WAS BEING SPENT TO FEED THE HIDERS.

**WILLEM VAN MAAREN,** THE WAREHOUSE MANAGER, **DIDN'T** KNOW ABOUT THE PEOPLE HIDING, BUT BEGAN TO SUSPECT...

HE LEFT SHEETS OF PAPER HANGING OFF THE EDGE OF DESKS AS **BOOBY TRAPS**. IF THEY WERE DISTURBED, HE'D KNOW SOMEONE HAD BEEN THERE.

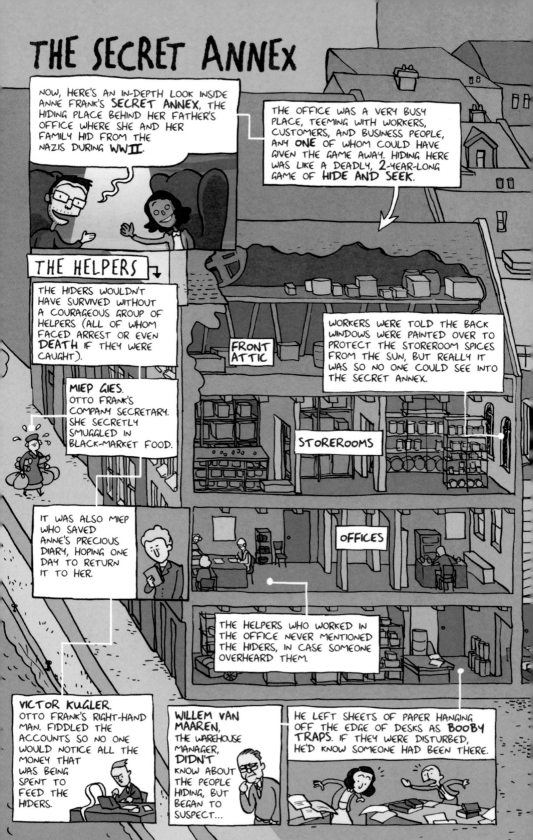

**ANNE FRANK.** THE WRITER OF THE DIARY. KNOWN AS A LIGHTHEARTED JOKER WITH A SERIOUS AND CONTEMPLATIVE SIDE.

**OTTO FRANK.** ANNE'S FATHER. THE LEADER OF THE GROUP. THE SECRET ANNEX IS HIS IDEA.

**EDITH FRANK.** ANNE'S MOTHER. ANNE FINDS HER HARSH AND UNSYMPATHETIC.

**MARGOT FRANK.** ANNE'S OLDER SISTER. QUIET AND SERIOUS. SPENDS A LOT OF TIME STUDYING.

**HERMANN VAN PELS.** THE HANDYMAN OF THE HOUSE. OPTIMISTIC AND UPBEAT, AT LEAST UNTIL HIS CIGARETTES RUN OUT...

**AUGUSTE VAN PELS.** THE COOK OF THE HOUSE. LOVES TO CAUSE ARGUMENTS.

**PETER VAN PELS.** QUIET AND SHY. ANNE THINKS SHE HAS FALLEN IN LOVE WITH PETER, BUT LATER SUSPECTS IT'S JUST THE EFFECT OF BEING COOPED UP.

**FRITZ PFEFFER.** ANNE'S ROOMMATE. HE IS IN HIDING WITHOUT HIS FIANCÉE, WHOM HE WORRIES ABOUT CONSTANTLY. IT MAY BE THIS THAT MAKES MAKES HIM SO IRRITATING!

DURING THE DAY, THEY HID IN THE CRAMPED SECRET ANNEX. AT NIGHT THEY COULD STRETCH THEIR LEGS IN THE FRONT OFFICE, BUT NEVER OUTSIDE!

ANNE LOVED TO LOOK OUT FROM THE **ATTIC WINDOW** AT THE MOON AND THE BIG CHESTNUT TREE IN THE NEIGHBORS' GARDEN.

THE ENTRANCE WAS THROUGH A **HIDDEN DOOR** BEHIND A BOOKCASE.

AUGUSTE AND HERMANN'S ROOM (ALSO THE DINING ROOM)

PETER'S ROOM

OTTO, EDITH, AND MARGOT'S ROOM

ANNE AND FRITZ'S ROOM

THE **OFFICE KITCHEN** WAS THE ONLY PLACE IN THE BUILDING WITH HOT WATER, THE HIDERS HAD TO SNEAK DOWN HERE WHEN THE OFFICE WAS CLOSED TO GET WATER FOR WASHING.

WAREHOUSE

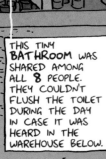

THIS TINY **BATHROOM** WAS SHARED AMONG ALL **8** PEOPLE. THEY COULDN'T FLUSH THE TOILET DURING THE DAY IN CASE IT WAS HEARD IN THE WAREHOUSE BELOW.

THE **BACK CURTAINS** OF THE ANNEX HAD TO BE KEPT DRAWN AT ALL TIMES, FOR FEAR OF BEING SEEN AND REPORTED BY A NEIGHBOR. THIS ALSO MEANT THE WINDOWS HAD TO BE KEPT SHUT, EVEN ON THE HOTTEST DAYS.

MY FINAL GUEST IS A **SUPERSONIC SUPERSTAR** WHOSE EXTRAORDINARY STORY OF RAGS TO RICHES TO RAGS AGAIN, TO RICHES AGAIN, **SCORCHED A TRAIL** FOR EVERY SUBSEQUENT CELEBRITY TO FOLLOW.

QUEEN OF THE CHORUS LINE, DARLING OF THE JAZZ AGE, SOCIAL JUSTICE WARRIOR, AND NAZI-SMASHING SPY! GET READY FOR THE **ROLLER-COASTER** LIFE OF...

# JOSEPHINE BAKER!

JOSEPHINE BAKER

ENTERTAINER 1906-1975

MS. BAKER, YOUR COURAGE, DETERMINATION, AND **RAW TALENT** CATAPULTED YOU FROM POVERTY TO SUPERSTARDOM. WHAT MADE YOU WANT TO GO INTO SHOW BUSINESS?

WELL, I'D ALWAYS LOVED DANCING AND MAKING PEOPLE LAUGH. I USED TO PUT ON LITTLE SHOWS FOR THE LOCAL KIDS BACK IN MY HOMETOWN OF **ST. LOUIS, MISSOURI.**

BUT MY MOM WANTED ME TO GET A **REAL** JOB—SO SHE SENT ME TO WORK AS A LIVE-IN MAID FOR A RICH WHITE FAMILY.

114

THEY BEAT ME, INSULTED ME, AND MADE ME SLEEP ON THE FLOOR WITH THE DOG. BACK THEN, THAT SORT OF THING WAS HAPPENING TO BLACK PEOPLE ALL OVER THE PLACE.

HOW **VILE!**

AFTER THAT, I SWORE **NOTHING,** ESPECIALLY NOT SOME **RACIST IDIOTS,** WAS GOING TO STOP ME FROM LIVING LIFE TO THE FULLEST.

ONE DAY I STOPPED TO DANCE WITH SOME STREET PERFORMERS, JUST FOR FUN. A LOCAL THEATER MANAGER SPOTTED US, LIKED MY STYLE, AND DECIDED TO HIRE US FOR HIS SHOW.

THAT LUCKY BREAK LAUNCHED YOUR RISE TO FAME. FROM STREET PERFORMER TO CHORUS GIRL TO BROADWAY STAR, WHEREVER YOU WENT, PEOPLE FELL IN LOVE WITH YOUR INFECTIOUS BLEND OF HIGH-ENERGY CHARLESTON DANCING AND SLAPSTICK COMEDY.

YEAH, BUT NO MATTER HOW SUCCESSFUL I GOT, I WAS STILL SURROUNDED BY PEOPLE WHO LOOKED DOWN ON ME BECAUSE OF MY SKIN COLOR.

IMAGINE! I COULD PLAY TO A SOLD-OUT NIGHTCLUB, BUT I COULDN'T EVEN GET A CUP OF COFFEE AFTERWARD, BECAUSE THE WAITER THOUGHT IT WAS "BENEATH HIM" TO SERVE A BLACK PERSON!

SO WHEN THE OPPORTUNITY CAME UP TO GO TO **PARIS** AS THE STAR OF FRANCE'S FIRST ALL-BLACK MUSICAL, YOU JUMPED AT THE CHANCE!

PARIS WAS LIKE A DIFFERENT WORLD! THEY HAD NONE OF THE NO-BLACK-PEOPLE LAWS THAT HAD DRIVEN ME NUTS IN THE STATES. I COULD GET COFFEE WHEREVER I LIKED!

AND IT WAS THERE THAT YOU TRULY BECAME A SUPERSTAR. YOUR "DANSE SAUVAGE," PERFORMED COMPLETELY NUDE EXCEPT FOR A STRING OF BANANAS, MADE YOU AN **ICON** OF THE JAZZ AGE.

ALTHOUGH, UM... IS THAT REALLY MUCH BETTER? I MEAN, THAT'S **HORRENDOUSLY RACIST,** RIGHT?

WHAT? THE BANANA SKIRT? OH, YES, OF COURSE.

BUT LOOK, HERE'S THE THING. I DIDN'T HAVE A CHOICE BETWEEN RACISM AND NO RACISM. IT WAS EVERYWHERE. I HAD A CHOICE BETWEEN BEING LEGALLY **SHUT OUT** OF SOCIETY, OR BEING **CELEBRATED,** BUT IN AN IGNORANT, RACIST WAY.

THAT DOESN'T MAKE IT ANY LESS INSULTING, BUT I DID WHAT I HAD TO, TO BUILD A BETTER LIFE. AND OVER TIME, I STARTED TO CHANGE MY IMAGE, CHALLENGING MY AUDIENCES' OFFENSIVE IDEAS ABOUT BLACK PEOPLE.

I REINVENTED MYSELF AS A SOPHISTICATED, HIGH-SOCIETY LADY. I EVEN HIRED A DOWN-AND-OUT **COUNTESS** TO TEACH ME FANCY MANNERS.

THEN, **YOU** SAY "CHAARMED..."

CHAARMED.

YOUR UNCANNY ABILITY TO PLAY THE FAME GAME MADE YOU THE DARLING OF STYLISH SOCIETY. SUDDENLY, YOU WERE HOBNOBBING WITH POETS, PAINTERS, POLITICIANS, AND PRINCESSES!

WAS THAT A... **CHEETAH?**

AH, YES, DEAR CHIQUITA THE CHEETAH. I KEPT HER AS A PET...

**FABULOUS** PUBLICITY, YOU KNOW...

UNTIL SHE ESCAPED FROM MY CASTLE AND SCARED SOME OLD LADY HALF TO DEATH, AND I HAD TO GIVE HER BACK TO THE ZOO.

OH, DID I MENTION I BOUGHT A CASTLE...? AH, YES, GOOD TIMES...

YOU WERE THE MOST FAMOUS, MOST PHOTOGRAPHED, BEST-PAID WOMAN IN EUROPE.

BUT THEN, WHEN WWII BROKE OUT, I DECIDED TO USE MY CELEBRITY STATUS TO HELP THE **FRENCH RESISTANCE**, THE SECRET ARMY OF SPIES AND SABOTEURS FIGHTING THE NAZIS **INSIDE** OCCUPIED FRANCE.

I SMUGGLED SECRET MESSAGES WRITTEN IN **INVISIBLE INK** ON MY SHEETS OF MUSIC.

I'M TERRIBLY SORRY, FRAULEIN BAKER.

CAN I STILL GET AN AUTOGRAPH?

HMPH.

FRANCE GAVE ME A BUNCH OF MEDALS FOR THAT AFTER THE WAR.

AND YOUR NAZI-SMASHING EXPLOITS INSPIRED YOU TO TRY FIGHTING INJUSTICE AT HOME...

I STARTED TO SPEAK OUT ABOUT THE WAY THE UNITED STATES WAS TREATING ITS BLACK PEOPLE, JOINING THE GROWING MOVEMENT TO GET THOSE RACIST LAWS CHANGED.

AND I BEGAN AN AMERICA-WIDE TOUR, FORCING ANYWHERE I PLAYED TO TREAT BLACK AND WHITE PEOPLE EQUALLY.

FINE. I'LL JUST GO SOMEWHERE ELSE...

NO, WAIT!

THEATER

WHITES ONLY

I MEAN, IT SEEMED TO ME THAT IF BLACK AND WHITE PEOPLE COULDN'T HAVE **FUN** TOGETHER, HOW WOULD THEY EVER LEARN TO GET ALONG?

AND SO YOU BEGAN YOUR MOST AMBITIOUS **EVERYONE-GETTING-ALONG** PROJECT YET: **THE RAINBOW TRIBE.**

A MASSIVE FAMILY OF ADOPTED ORPHANS (**12** IN TOTAL) FROM ALL OVER THE WORLD, EACH RAISED IN THE TRADITIONAL CULTURE OF THEIR HOMELAND, AND ALL LIVING AND PLAYING TOGETHER IN YOUR CHATEAU, NOW CONVERTED INTO A JOSEPHINE-BAKER-THEMED **AMUSEMENT PARK!**

A GLORIOUS LIVING EXAMPLE OF **MULTI-RACIAL INTEGRATION** IN ONE BIG HAPPY, **TOURIST-ATTRACTION** FAMILY!

UM, IS THAT REALLY OK? IT SEEMS KINDA LIKE A **HUMAN ZOO?** WERE THE KIDS ALL RIGHT WITH BEING DRESSED UP AND PARADED AROUND LIKE THAT?

WELL, NO FAMILY'S **PERFECT.** AS FAR AS I'M CONCERNED, THE PROBLEMS ONLY **REALLY** STARTED WHEN THE **MONEY** RAN OUT...

IT WASN'T **CHEAP** BEING JOSEPHINE BAKER. PLUS OF COURSE THE COST OF THE CASTLE—THE SERVANTS, THE TUTORS, THE ZOO, ALL THOSE **NANNIES**...

IN THE END, WE WERE SO FAR IN DEBT WE GOT **EVICTED.** THE FAMILY WERE BROKEN UP, WITH SOME GOING TO STAY WITH FRIENDS AND RELATIVES...

I WAS **DESTITUTE**— RELYING ON THE KINDNESS OF CELEBRITY FRIENDS TO KEEP ME FROM STARVING.

BUT YOUR WILD RIDE OF A LIFE DOESN'T END THERE. **50** YEARS AFTER YOUR TRIUMPHAL ENTRANCE INTO PARIS, YOU ORGANISED A COMEBACK!

A SINGLE, SUPERB, SOLD-OUT, STAR-STUDDED, STANDING-OVATION-INSPIRING PERFORMANCE JUST DAYS BEFORE YOU DIED.

DID YOU KNOW FRANCE HONOURED YOU WITH A **21**-GUN SALUTE AT YOUR FUNERAL?

THAT'S WHAT I CALL GOING OUT WITH A BANG!

# DANCE THE CHARLESTON

DANCE SUPERSTAR **JOSEPHINE BAKER** TOOK THE WORLD BY STORM WITH HER CROWD-CONQUERING **CHARLESTON**. I'VE ASKED HER TO SHOW US HOW IT'S DONE...

WITH PLEASURE!

LET'S START WITH THE BASICS AND THEN WE'LL BUILD IN SOME DIFFERENT MOVEMENTS.

YOU'RE GOING TO BE SLIDING YOUR FEET AROUND A LOT, SO MAKE SURE YOU HAVE SLIPPERY-SOLED SHOES.

## STAGE 1: THE WALK

OR ELSE DANCE IN YOUR SOCKS!

## STAGE 3: NOW PUT THEM ALL TOGETHER!

**1** LEFT FOOT STEP, SWIVEL HEELS IN.

AND

AS YOU STEP THE RIGHT FOOT FORWARD, SWIVEL YOUR HEELS **OUT** AND YOUR KNEES **IN** ON BOTH LEGS (THIS IS WHILE YOUR FOOT IS IN THE AIR).

**2** RIGHT FOOT TAP FORWARD, SWIVEL HEELS IN.

## STAGE 5: THE KNEE THING

THESE STEPS ARE **SO FUN**, YOU CAN DO THEM OVER AND OVER. OR YOU CAN MIX IN SOME OTHER MOVES, LIKE...

**1** PUT YOUR HANDS FLAT ON YOUR KNEES. BEND YOUR KNEES OUT.

**2** PUT YOUR KNEES TOGETHER AND SLIDE YOUR HANDS ONE OVER THE OTHER.

**3** SLIDE YOUR KNEES BACK OUT, BUT THIS TIME KEEP YOUR HAND ON THE OPPOSITE KNEE.

**4** KNEES AND HANDS TOGETHER AGAIN.

## 1  STEP FORWARD WITH YOUR LEFT FOOT.

## 2  STEP FORWARD AND JUST **TAP** THE TOES OF YOUR RIGHT FOOT.

## 3  STEP YOUR RIGHT FOOT BACK.

## 4  STEP BACK AND TAP YOUR LEFT FOOT.

PRACTICE THAT FOR A BIT (TRY DOING IT TO MUSIC), THEN LET'S ADD...

# STAGE 2: THE SWIVELS

## 1  SWIVEL YOUR HEELS **IN** AND YOUR KNEES **OUT**.

## 2  SWIVEL YOUR HEELS **OUT** AND YOUR KNEES **IN**.

AND AS YOU STEP BACK, SWIVEL HEELS OUT AGAIN.

## 3  SWIVEL HEELS IN.

AND OUT.

## 4  IN.

AND OUT.

NOW YOU'RE GETTING IT!

# STAGE 4: ADD THE ARMS!

SWING ARMS RIGHT ON EACH LEFT FOOT STEP.

SWING LEFT ON EACH RIGHT STEP.

ADD A BIT OF A **HEAD WOBBLE** FOR EXTRA FLAPPER POINTS!

TO **REALLY** GET YOUR CHARLESTON ON, YOU'LL NEED SOME **PROPER** JAZZ DANCING MUSIC. YOU COULD TRY:

**SUGAR** BY BILLIE HOLIDAY
**SMOOTH**—A GOOD PRACTICE TRACK.

**MINOR SWING** BY DJANGO REINHARDT AND STÉPHANE GRAPPELLI
**HOT**—A SMOKIN' PARIS JAZZ NUMBER.

**THE CHARLESTON** BY SPIKE JONES AND HIS CITY SLICKERS
**INSANE!** JUST TRY AND KEEP UP!

THAT'S IT! YOU'RE NOW A CHARLESTON CHAMPION!

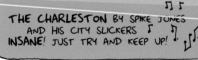

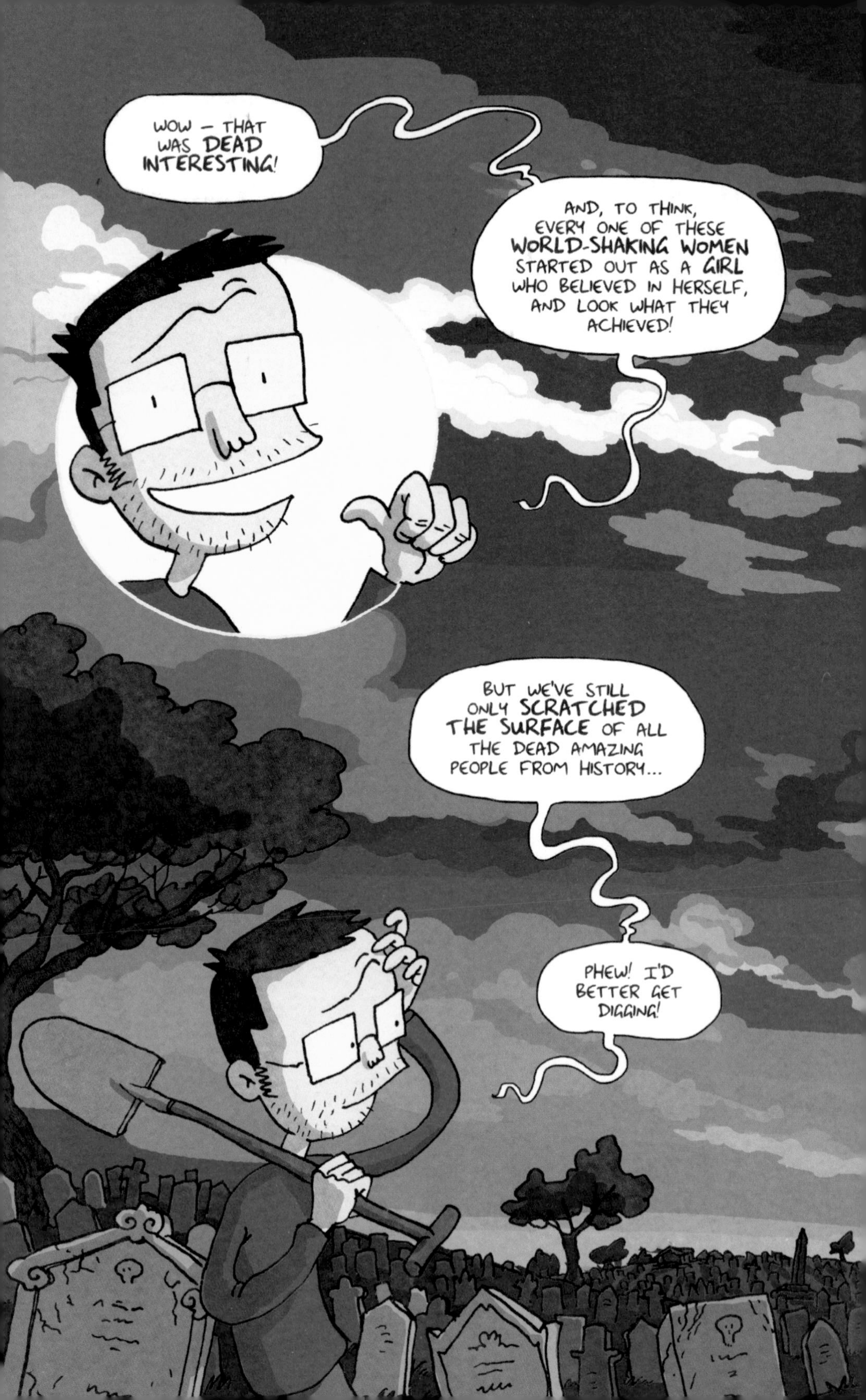
WOW – THAT WAS DEAD INTERESTING!
AND, TO THINK, EVERY ONE OF THESE WORLD-SHAKING WOMEN STARTED OUT AS A GIRL WHO BELIEVED IN HERSELF, AND LOOK WHAT THEY ACHIEVED!
BUT WE'VE STILL ONLY SCRATCHED THE SURFACE OF ALL THE DEAD AMAZING PEOPLE FROM HISTORY...
PHEW! I'D BETTER GET DIGGING!

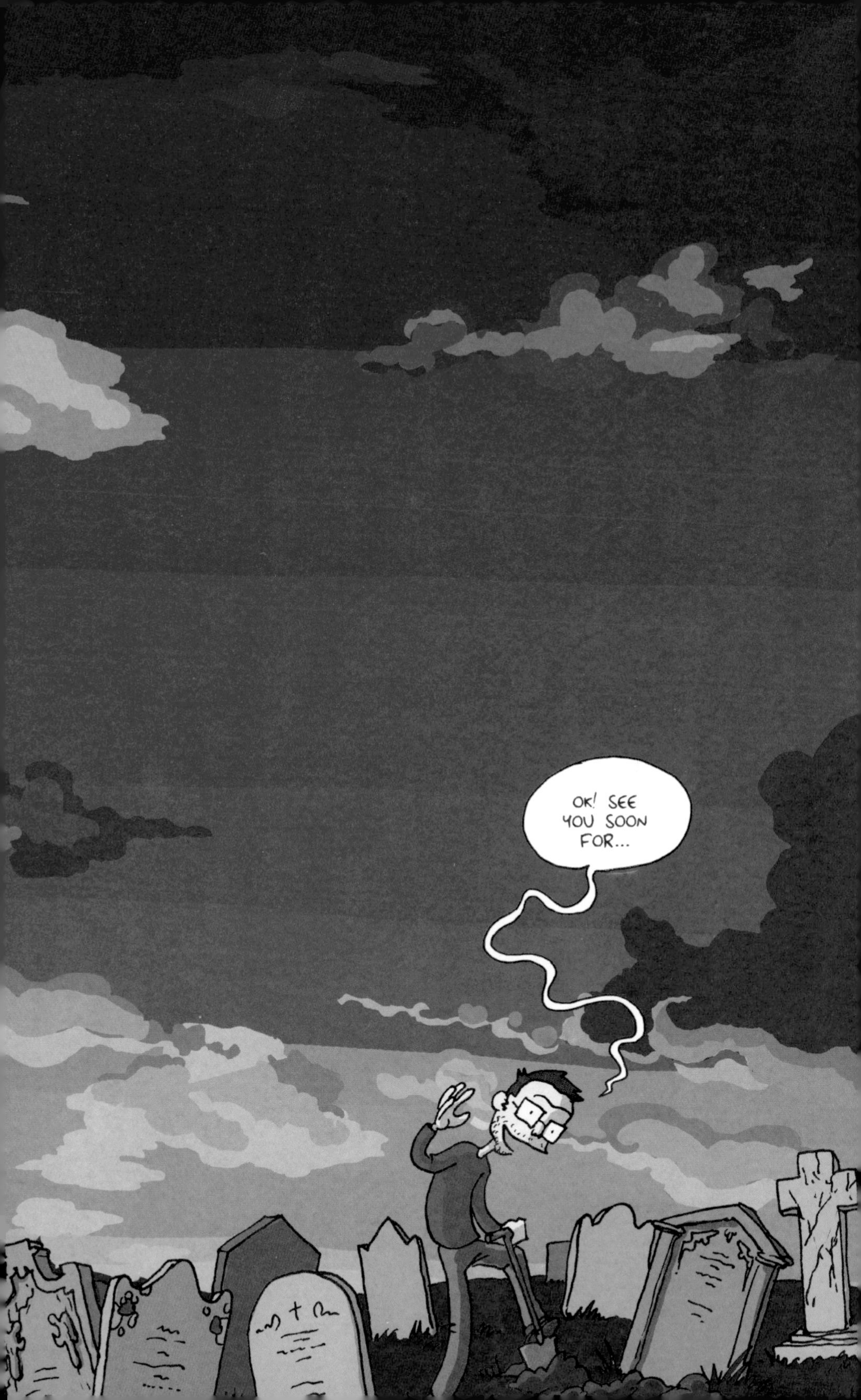
OK! SEE YOU SOON FOR...

# OUT NOW

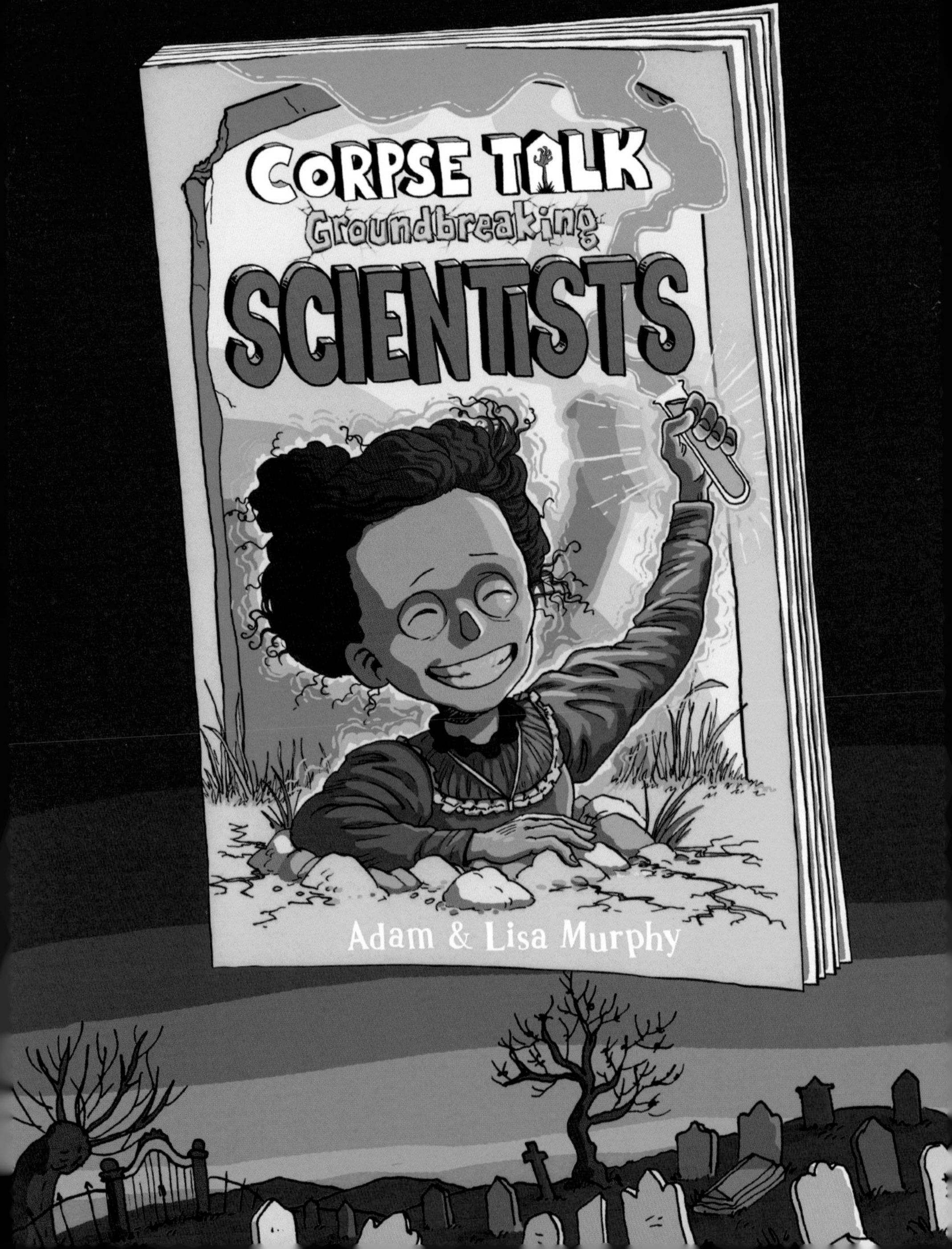
CORPSE TALK
Groundbreaking
SCIENTISTS
Adam & Lisa Murphy

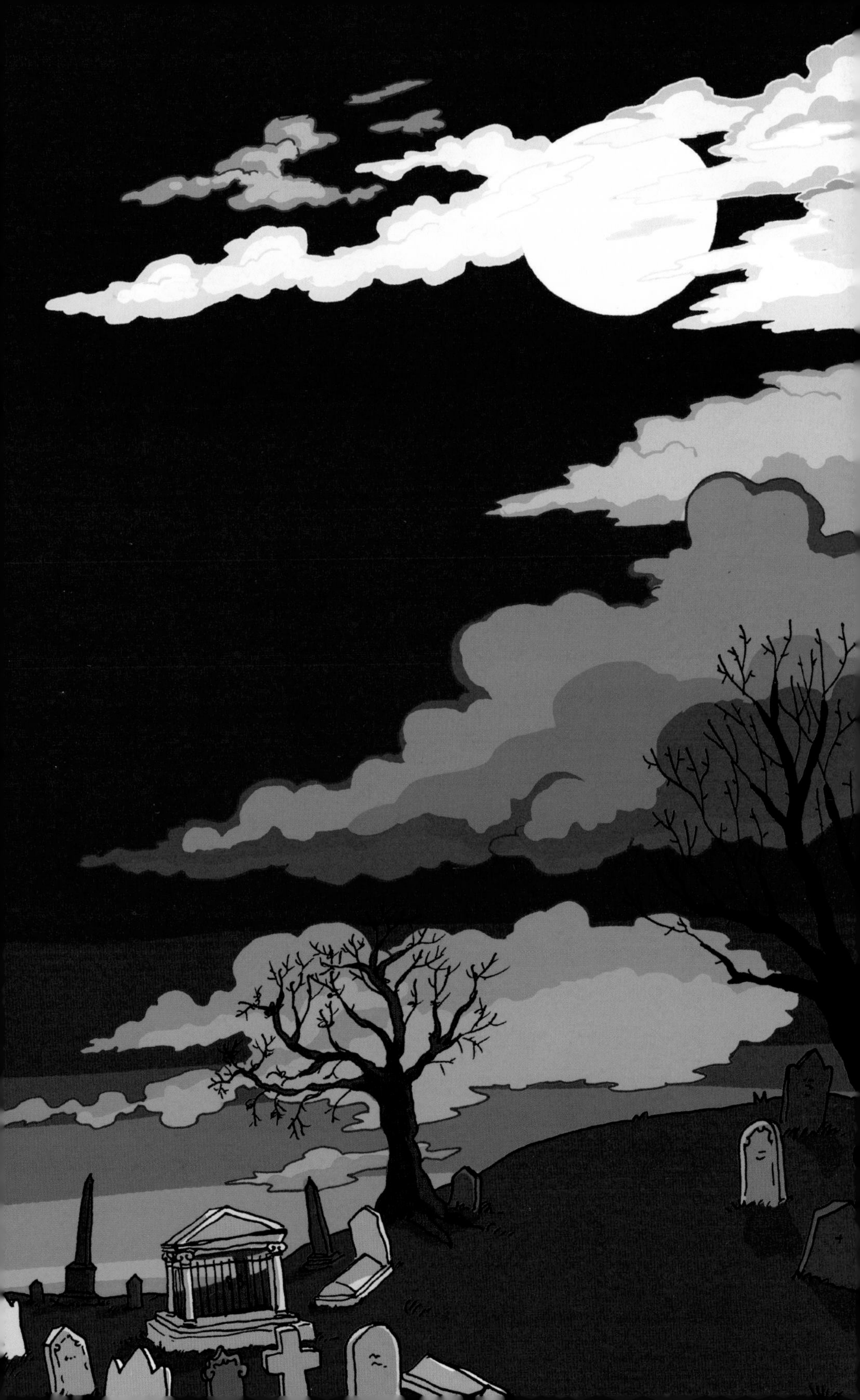

# Glossary

**ABOLITIONIST** SOMEONE WHO WANTS TO ABOLISH (GET RID OF) SLAVERY.

**ALLIANCE** WHEN TWO OR MORE COUNTRIES TEAM UP TO HELP EACH OTHER OUT.

**ARMADA** A LARGE FLEET OF WARSHIPS.

**AVIATOR** SOMEONE WHO FLIES AIRPLANES; ALSO KNOWN AS A PILOT.

**BIPLANE** A PLANE THAT HAS TWO WINGS ON EACH SIDE, ONE FIXED ABOVE THE OTHER. BIPLANES WERE COMMON IN THE EARLY 20TH CENTURY.

**BUCCANEER** A PIRATE WHO OPERATED IN THE CARIBBEAN.

**BYZANTIUM** AN ANCIENT GREEK CITY; TODAY IT IS CALLED ISTANBUL AND IS LOCATED IN TURKEY.

**CHARLESTON** A POPULAR DANCE IN THE 1920S.

**CONCENTRATION CAMPS** CAMPS, OFTEN USED DURING TIMES OF WAR, WHERE PEOPLE ARE HELD AGAINST THEIR WILL ON ACCOUNT OF THEIR RACE, GENDER, SEXUAL ORIENTATION, OR POLITICAL BELIEFS; USUALLY ASSOCIATED WITH THE NAZI WAR CAMPS OF WORLD WAR II.

**DESTITUTE** TO BE SO POOR THAT YOU CANNOT CARE FOR YOUR OWN WELL-BEING.

**ENGINEERING** THE PROFESSION OF DESIGNING AND CREATING VEHICLES, STRUCTURES, MACHINES, AND OTHER TECHNOLOGIES.

**THE ENLIGHTENMENT** A PHILOSOPHICAL REVOLUTION DURING THE 18TH CENTURY WHERE THINKERS CHAMPIONED REASON OVER SUPERSTITION.

**GENOCIDE**  THE MASS MURDER OF A PARTICULAR GROUP OF PEOPLE.

**GUILLOTINE**  A HEAVY-BLADED MACHINE FOR BEHEADING PEOPLE, INVENTED DURING THE FRENCH REVOLUTION.

**THE HOLOCAUST**  THE SYSTEMATIC MURDER OF JEWISH PEOPLE BY NAZI GERMANY IN THE YEARS **1939—1945**, DURING WORLD WAR II.

**HUNDRED YEARS' WAR**  A SERIES OF BATTLES FOUGHT OVER **116** YEARS (IRONICALLY), FOR THE RIGHT TO RULE FRANCE.

**JOURNALIST**  SOMEONE WHO REPORTS THE NEWS.

**JUNK**  A TYPE OF ANCIENT CHINESE SAILING SHIP; STILL USED TODAY.

**LIFT**  THE FORCE REQUIRED TO MAKE AN AIRPLANE, OR BIRD, TAKE OFF.

**MILLENIA**  SEVERAL THOUSAND YEARS—IS THE PLURAL OF MILLENNIUM, WHICH MEANS **1,000** YEARS.

**NEOPLATONISTS**  A GROUP OF ANCIENT PHILOSOPHERS WHO FOLLOWED THE TEACHINGS OF **PLATO**. THEY BELIEVED ALL OF REALITY ORIGINATED FROM A SINGLE, PERFECT, UNKNOWABLE SOURCE THAT THEY CALLED "THE ONE".

**PHILOSOPHY** A METHOD OF TRYING TO UNDERSTAND THE WORLD BY ASKING A LOT OF QUESTIONS.

**POPE** THE HEAD OF THE ROMAN CATHOLIC CHURCH.

**RACISM** ACTS OF SUBTLE OR OVERT HATRED AND HOSTILITY TOWARD OTHER PEOPLE BASED SOLELY ON THEIR ETHNIC BACKGROUND.

**SENSATIONALISM** TO PRESENT A STORY IN A MANNER THAT EXAGGERATES THE TRUTH FOR EFFECT.

**SEXISM** ACTS OF SUBTLE OR OVERT HOSTILITY OR DISCRIMINATION TOWARD OTHER PEOPLE BASED SOLELY ON THEIR GENDER.

**SILK ROAD** A HISTORIC NETWORK OF TRADE ROUTES LINKING EUROPE AND ASIA; NAMED AFTER THE SILK GOODS THAT WERE TRADED ALONG ITS ROUTE.

**SUFFRAGETTE** A MEMBER OF THE MILITANT MOVEMENT WHO FOUGHT FOR WOMEN'S RIGHTS AT THE START OF THE 20TH CENTURY.

**THE TUDORS** ROYAL FAMILY WHO RULED ENGLAND, IRELAND, AND WALES FROM 1485 TO 1603. MEMBERS OF THE TUDOR FAMILY INCLUDED HENRY VIII AND ELIZABETH I.

**TYPHOON** A SEVERE TROPICAL STORM LOCATED IN THE WEST PACIFIC OCEAN.

**UNDERGROUND RAILROAD**
A SECRET NETWORK OF PEOPLE
AND SAFE HOUSES, STARTED IN THE
LATE **18**TH CENTURY, THAT HELPED
ENSLAVED AFRICAN PEOPLE ESCAPE
FROM THE SLAVE STATES IN THE
SOUTHERN **US** TO FREE STATES IN
THE NORTH, AND CANADA.

**WORLD WAR II**  A GLOBAL
CONFLICT THAT TOOK PLACE
BETWEEN **1939** AND **1945**.

Penguin Random House

For Elizabeth, Ara, Anne, Madelyn, Peggy, Vera.
Women who shaped us. We miss you fiercely.

**Design and adaptation** Paul Duffield
**Additional colour flatting** David B Cooper
**With special thanks to** Tom Fickling,
Anthony Hinton, and Joe Brady
**US Senior Editor** Shannon Beatty
**US Editor** Margaret Parrish
**Senior Production Editor** Nikoleta Parasaki
**Senior Production Controller** Inderjit Bhullar
**Publishing Director** Sarah Larter

First American Edition, 2020
Published in the United States by DK Publishing
1450 Broadway, Suite 801, New York, NY 10018

DK, a Division of Penguin Random House LLC
20 21 22 23 24 10 9 8 7 6 5 4 3 2 1
001–315772–Aug/2020

Published in Great Britain by Dorling Kindersley Limited

A catalog record for this book
is available from the Library of Congress.
ISBN: 978-1-4654-9977-6 (Paperback)
ISBN: 978-0-7440-2357-2 (Hardback)

DK books are available at special discounts when purchased
in bulk for sales promotions, premiums, fund-raising, or
educational use. For details, contact:
DK Publishing Special Markets,
1450 Broadway, Suite 801, New York, NY 10018
SpecialSales@dk.com

Printed and bound in the USA.

For the curious
**www.dk.com**